Cisco Networking Academy Program
CCNP 2: Remote Access Lab Companion
Second Edition

Cisco Systems, Inc.
Cisco Networking Academy Program

Cisco Press
800 East 96th Street
Indianapolis, IN 46240 USA

Cisco Networking Academy Program
CCNP 2: Remote Access Lab Companion
Second Edition

Cisco Systems, Inc.
Cisco Networking Academy Program

Copyright © 2004 Cisco Systems, Inc.

Published by:
Cisco Press
800 East 96th Street
Indianapolis, Indiana 46240 USA

Printed in the United States of America   1 2 3 4 5 6 7 8 9 0

First Printing   April 2004

ISBN: 1-58713-146-3

Warning and Disclaimer

This book is designed to provide information based on content from the Cisco Networking Academy Program *CCNP 2: Remote Access* course. Every effort has been made to make this book as complete and as accurate as possible, but no warranty or fitness is implied.

The information is provided on an "as is" basis. The author, Cisco Press, and Cisco Systems, Inc., shall have neither liability nor responsibility to any person or entity with respect to any loss or damages arising from the information contained in this book or from the use of the programs that may accompany it.

The opinions expressed in this book belong to the author and are not necessarily those of Cisco Systems, Inc.

This book is part of the Cisco Networking Academy® Program series from Cisco Press. The products in this
CISCO SYSTEMS **series support and complement the Cisco Networking Academy Program curriculum. If you are using this book outside the Networking Academy program, then you are not preparing with a Cisco trained and authorized Networking Academy provider.**

For information on the Cisco Networking Academy Program or to locate a Networking Academy, please visit www.cisco.com/edu.

Trademark Acknowledgments

All terms mentioned in this book that are known to be trademarks or service marks have been appropriately capitalized. Cisco Press or Cisco Systems, Inc., cannot attest to the accuracy of this information. Use of a term in this book should not be regarded as affecting the validity of any trademark or service mark.

Corporate and Government Sales

Cisco Press offers excellent discounts on this book when ordered in quantity for bulk purchases or special sales. For more information, please contact:

U.S. Corporate and Government Sales 1-800-382-3419 corpsales@pearsontechgroup.com

For sales outside the U.S., please contact: International Sales international@pearsoned.com

Feedback Information

At Cisco Press, our goal is to create in-depth technical books of the highest quality and value. Each book is crafted with care and precision, undergoing rigorous development that involves the unique expertise of members of the professional technical community.

Readers' feedback is a natural continuation of this process. If you have any comments regarding how we could improve the quality of this book, or otherwise alter it to better suit your needs, you can contact us at networkingacademy@ciscopress.com. Please be sure to include the book title and ISBN in your message.

We greatly appreciate your assistance.

Publisher	John Wait
Editor-in-Chief	John Kane
Executive Editor	Mary Beth Ray
Cisco Systems Representative	Anthony Wolfenden
Cisco Press Program Manager	Nannette M. Noble
Production Manager	Patrick Kanouse
Development Editor	Dayna Isley
Technical Editors	K Kirkendall, Jim Lorenz
Senior Project Editor	Sheri Cain
Copy Editor	Kris Simmons

CISCO SYSTEMS

Corporate Headquarters
Cisco Systems, Inc.
170 West Tasman Drive
San Jose, CA 95134-1706
USA
www.cisco.com
Tel: 408 526-4000
    800 553-NETS (6387)
Fax: 408 526-4100

European Headquarters
Cisco Systems International BV
Haarlerbergpark
Haarlerbergweg 13-19
1101 CH Amsterdam
The Netherlands
www-europe.cisco.com
Tel: 31 0 20 357 1000
Fax: 31 0 20 357 1100

Americas Headquarters
Cisco Systems, Inc.
170 West Tasman Drive
San Jose, CA 95134-1706
USA
www.cisco.com
Tel: 408 526-7660
Fax: 408 527-0883

Asia Pacific Headquarters
Cisco Systems, Inc.
Capital Tower
168 Robinson Road
#22-01 to #29-01
Singapore 068912
www.cisco.com
Tel: +65 6317 7777
Fax: +65 6317 7799

Cisco Systems has more than 200 offices in the following countries and regions. Addresses, phone numbers, and fax numbers are listed on the
Cisco.com Web site at www.cisco.com/go/offices.

Argentina • Australia • Austria • Belgium • Brazil • Bulgaria • Canada • Chile • China PRC • Colombia • Costa Rica • Croatia • Czech Republic
Denmark • Dubai, UAE • Finland • France • Germany • Greece • Hong Kong SAR • Hungary • India • Indonesia • Ireland • Israel • Italy
Japan • Korea • Luxembourg • Malaysia • Mexico • The Netherlands • New Zealand • Norway • Peru • Philippines • Poland • Portugal
Puerto Rico • Romania • Russia • Saudi Arabia • Scotland • Singapore • Slovakia • Slovenia • South Africa • Spain • Sweden
Switzerland • Taiwan • Thailand • Turkey • Ukraine • United Kingdom • United States • Venezuela • Vietnam • Zimbabwe

About the Technical Editors

K Kirkendall is a teacher at Boise State University in Boise, Idaho, where he teaches Cisco, Microsoft, and network security courses. For the last six years, K has also worked for the Networking Academy in the assessment division, which writes questions for the Cisco Networking Academy Program and Cisco Certification exams. K has a B.A. from St. Leo College in Business Administration and is working on his MIS degree at Boise State. He has several industry certifications, including CCNP, CCNA, CCAI, CCDA, MCP, CNA, A+, Network+, and Server+. K and his wonderful and understanding wife, Jeanine, have five wonderful children and two super grandsons.

Jim Lorenz is an instructor and curriculum developer for the Cisco Networking Academy Program. He has more than 20 years of experience in information systems and has held various IT positions in Fortune 500 companies, including Honeywell and Motorola. Jim has developed and taught computer and networking courses for both public and private institutions for more than 15 years. He is co-author of the Cisco Networking Academy Program Fundamentals of UNIX course, contributing author for the CCNA Lab Companion manuals, and technical editor for the CCNA Companion Guides. Jim is a Cisco Certified Academy Instructor (CCAI) for CCNA and CCNP courses. He has a bachelor's degree in computer information systems and is currently working on his masters in information networking and telecommunications. Jim and his wife, Mary, have two daughters, Jessica and Natasha.

Table of Contents

Foreword

Throughout the world, the Internet has brought tremendous new opportunities for individuals and their employers. Companies and other organizations are seeing dramatic increases in productivity by investing in robust networking capabilities. Some studies have shown measurable productivity improvements in entire economies. The promise of enhanced efficiency, profitability, and standard of living is real and growing.

Such productivity gains aren't achieved by simply purchasing networking equipment. Skilled professionals are needed to plan, design, install, deploy, configure, operate, maintain, and troubleshoot today's networks. Network managers must ensure that they have planned for network security and for continued operation. They need to design for the required performance level in their organization. They must implement new capabilities as the demands of their organization, and its reliance on the network, expands.

To meet the many educational needs of the internetworking community, Cisco Systems established the Cisco Networking Academy Program. The Networking Academy is a comprehensive learning program that provides students with the Internet technology skills essential in a global economy. The Networking Academy integrates face-to-face teaching, web-based content, online assessment, student performance tracking, hands-on labs, instructor training and support, and preparation for industry-standard certifications.

The Networking Academy continually raises the bar on blended learning and educational processes. All instructors are Cisco Certified Academy Instructors (CCAIs). The Internet-based assessment and instructor support systems are some of the most extensive and validated ever developed, including a 24/7 customer service system for Networking Academy instructors and students. Through community feedback and electronic assessment, the Networking Academy adapts the curriculum to improve outcomes and student achievement. The Cisco Global Learning Network infrastructure designed for the Networking Academy delivers a rich, interactive, and personalized curriculum to students worldwide. The Internet has the power to change the way people work, live, play, and learn, and the Cisco Networking Academy Program is in the forefront of this transformation.

This Cisco Press title is one of a series of best-selling companion titles for the Cisco Networking Academy Program. Designed by Cisco Worldwide Education and Cisco Press, these books provide integrated support for the online learning content that is made available to Academies all over the world. These Cisco Press books are the only authorized books for the Networking Academy by Cisco Systems and provide print and CD-ROM materials that ensure the greatest possible learning experience for Networking Academy students.

I hope you are successful as you embark on your learning path with Cisco Systems and the Internet. I also hope that you will choose to continue your learning after you complete the Networking Academy curriculum. In addition to its Cisco Networking Academy Program titles, Cisco Press also publishes an extensive list of networking technology and certification publications that provide a wide range of resources. Cisco Systems has also established a network of professional training companies—the Cisco Learning Partners—who provide a full range of Cisco training courses. They offer training in many formats, including e-learning, self-paced, and instructor-led classes. Their instructors are Cisco certified, and Cisco creates their materials. When you are ready, please visit the Learning & Events area on Cisco.com to learn about all the educational support that Cisco and its partners have to offer.

Thank you for choosing this book and the Cisco Networking Academy Program.

Kevin Warner

Senior Director, Marketing
Worldwide Education
Cisco Systems, Inc.

Introduction

Cisco Networking Academy Program CCNP 2: Remote Access Lab Companion, Second Edition, supplements your classroom and laboratory experience with the Cisco Networking Academy Program.

This book contains all the labs in the current CCNP course within your Cisco Networking Academy Program. Most of the labs are hands-on and require access to a Cisco router or a lab simulator. Successful completion and understanding of the topics covered in the labs will help you to prepare for the Building Cisco Remote Access Networks exam (642-801), which is a qualifying exam for the Cisco Certified Network Professional (CCNP) certification.

The Audience of This Book

This book is written for anyone who wants to learn about Cisco remote-access technologies, especially students enrolled in the CCNP 2 Networking Academy course. Students in any educational environment could use this book as both a textbook companion and a lab manual.

How This Book Is Organized

Table I-1 outlines all the labs in this book, the corresponding Target Indicator (TI) in the online curriculum, and the time it should take to do the lab.

Table I-1   Master Lab Overview

Lab TI	Title	Estimated Time (Minutes)
1.5.1	Introductory Lab 1—Getting Started and Building Start.txt	30
1.5.2	Introductory Lab 2—Capturing HyperTerminal and Telnet Sessions	30
1.5.3	Introductory Lab 3—Access Control List Basics and Extended Ping	45
2.5.1	Configuring an Asynchronous Dialup Connection	35
2.5.2	Configuring an Asynchronous Dialup Connection on the AUX Port	25
2.5.3	Configuring an Asynchronous Dialup PPP	25

Lab TI	Title	Estimated Time (Minutes)
3.7.1	Configuring PPP Interactive Mode	30
3.7.2	Configuring PPP Options—Authentication and Compression	30
3.7.3	Configuring PPP Callback	30
4.9.1	Configuring ISDN BRI	50
4.9.2	Configuring Snapshot Routing	45
4.9.3	Using PPP Multilink for ISDN B Channel Aggregation	30
4.9.4	Configuring ISDN PRI	30
5.3.1	Configuring ISDN Using Dialer Profiles	45
5.3.2	Using a Dialer Map Class with Dialer Profiles	45
6.4.1	Basic Frame Relay Router and Switch Configuration	45
6.4.2	Configuring Full-Mesh Frame Relay	30
6.4.3	Configuring Full-Mesh Frame Relay with Subinterfaces	30
6.4.4	Configuring Hub-and-Spoke Frame Relay	30
7.3.1	Frame Relay Subinterfaces and Traffic Shaping	50
7.3.2	Frame Relay Traffic Shaping with Class-Based Weighted Fair Queuing	50
8.7.1	Configuring ISDN Dial Backup	45
8.7.2	Using Secondary Links for On-Demand Bandwidth	30

Lab TI	Title	Estimated Time (Minutes)
8.7.3	Configuring Dialer Backup with Dialer Profiles	45
8.7.4	Configuring DDR Backup Using BRIs and Dialer Watch	45
9.8.1	Managing Network Performance Using Class-Based Weighted Fair Queuing (CBWFQ) and Low Latency Queuing (LLQ)	45
10.5.1	Configuring Static NAT	30
10.5.2	Configuring Dynamic NAT	30
10.5.3	Configuring NAT Overload	45
10.5.4	Configuring TCP Load Distribution	25
11.3.1	Router Security and AAA Authentication	45
11.3.2	AAA Authorization and Accounting	45
11.3.3	AAA TACACS+ Server	25
13.8.1	Configuring a Site-to-Site IPSec VPN Using Preshared Keys	45

This Book's Features

Many of the book's features will help facilitate your full understanding of the networking and routing topics covered in the labs:

- **Objective**—Identifies the goal or goals that are to be accomplished in the lab.

- **Equipment Requirements**—Provides a list of the equipment to be used to run the lab.

- **Scenario**—Allows you to relate the lab exercise to real-world environments.

- **Questions**—As appropriate, labs include questions that are designed to elicit particular points of understanding. These questions help verify your comprehension of the technology being implemented.

The conventions used to present command syntax in this book are the same conventions used in the *Cisco IOS Command Reference*:

- **Bold** indicates commands and keywords that are entered literally as shown. In examples (not syntax), bold indicates user input (for example, a **show** command).

- *Italic* indicates arguments for which you supply values.

- Braces ({ }) indicate a required element.

- Square brackets ([ ]) indicate an optional element.

- Vertical bars (|) separate alternative, mutually exclusive elements.

- Braces and vertical bars within square brackets (such as [x {y | z}]) indicate a required choice within an optional element. You do not need to enter what is in the brackets, but if you do, you have some required choices in the braces.

Chapter 1

Wide-Area Networks

Lab 1.5.1: Introductory Lab 1—Getting Started and Building Start.txt

Estimated Time: 30 Minutes

Objective

This lab introduces new CCNP lab equipment and certain Cisco IOS features. This introductory activity also describes how to use a simple text editor to create all or part of a router configuration and apply that configuration to a router.

Equipment Requirements

The following equipment is required for this lab:

- A single router, preferably a 2600 series, and a workstation running a Windows operating system

- One 3 1/2-inch floppy disk with label

Preliminary Information

Modular Interfaces

Cisco routers can come with a variety of interface configurations. Some models have only fixed interfaces. Users cannot change or replace such interfaces. Other models have one or more modular interfaces. They allow the user to add, remove, or replace interfaces as needed.

Fixed interface identification, such as Serial 0, S0, and Ethernet 0, E0, might already be familiar. Modular routers use notation such as Serial 0/0 or S0/1, where the first number refers to the module and the second number refers to the interface. Both notations use 0 as their starting reference, so S0/1 indicates that there is another serial interface, S0/0.

Fast Ethernet

Many routers today are equipped with Fast Ethernet interfaces. Fast Ethernet has 10/100 Mbps autosensing. You must use Fast Ethernet 0/0 or Fa0/0 notation on routers with Fast Ethernet interfaces.

The **ip subnet-zero** *Command*

The **ip subnet-zero** command is enabled by default in IOS 12.0. This command lets you assign IP addresses in the first subnet, called subnet 0. Because subnet 0 uses only binary zeros in the subnet field, you might confuse its subnet address with the major network address. With the advent of classless IP, the use of subnet 0 has become more common. The labs in this manual assume that you can assign addresses to the router interfaces using subnet 0. If any routers have an IOS earlier than 12.0, you must add the global configuration command **ip subnet-zero** to the router configuration.

The **no shutdown** *Command*

Interfaces are shut down by default. Remember to type a **no shutdown** command in interface configuration mode when you are ready to bring up the interface. The command **no shutdown** does not appear in the output of the **show running-config** command.

Passwords

The **login** command is applied to virtual terminals by default. For the router to accept Telnet connections, you must configure a password. Otherwise, the router does not allow a Telnet connection, replying with the error message **password required, but none set**. You must also configure an enable secret password on the remote router to enter privileged mode after you establish a Telnet session. If there is no enable secret password on the remote router, it replies with the error message **% No password set**, and only user mode commands are available.

Step 1

Take a few moments to examine the router. Become familiar with any serial, Basic Rate Interface (BRI) (ISDN), Primary Rate Interface (PRI) (ISDN), and DSU/CSU interfaces on the router. Look closely at any connectors or cables that are not familiar.

Step 2

Establish a HyperTerminal session to the router. Enter privileged EXEC mode.

Step 3

To clear the configuration, issue the **erase startup-config** command.

Confirm the objective when prompted. The result should look something like this:

```
Router#erase startup-config
Erasing the nvram filesystem will remove all files! Continue? [confirm]
[OK]
Erase of nvram: complete
Router#
```

When the prompt returns, issue the **reload** command.

Answer **no** if asked to save changes and confirm the reload when prompted:

```
System configuration has been modified. Save? [yes/no]: no
Proceed with reload? [confirm]
```

After the router finishes the boot process, choose not to enter the system configuration dialog. Also, choose not to use the AutoInstall facility but press Enter to accept the default choice, which should be yes, as shown:

```
--- System Configuration Dialog ---
Would you like to enter the initial configuration dialog? [yes/no]: no
Would you like to terminate autoinstall? [yes]:
Press RETURN to get started!
```

Step 4

In privileged mode, issue the **show run** command.

Note the following default configurations while scrolling through the running configuration:

- The version number of the IOS.
- The **ip subnet-zero** command, which allows the use of subnet 0.
- Each available interface and its name.

*Note***:** Each interface has the **shutdown** command applied to its configuration.

- The **ip http server** command, which lets you access the router with a web browser. Some routers and IOS versions disable this feature by default using the **no ip http server** command.
- No passwords are set for CON, AUX, and VTY sessions, as shown here:

```
line con 0
transport input none
line aux 0
line vty 0 4
```

Note: The **transport input none** command is not applicable in Cisco IOS 12.2.

Using Copy and Paste with Notepad

In the next steps, use the copy and paste feature to edit router configurations. You must create a text file that you can paste into the routers and use as a starting point for the initial router configuration. Specifically, you must build a login configuration that you can use with every lab included in this manual.

Step 5

If necessary, issue the **show run** command again so that **line con** and **line vty** are showing on the screen:

```
line con 0
transport input none
line aux 0
line vty 0 4
!
end
```

Select the text as shown in this step and choose the **copy** command from HyperTerminal Edit menu.

Next, open Notepad. Notepad typically appears on the Start menu under Programs, Accessories. After Notepad opens, select **Paste** from the Notepad Edit menu.

Edit the lines in Notepad to look like the following lines. The one space indent is optional:

```
enable secret class
line con 0
 transport input none
 password cisco
 login
line aux 0
 password cisco
 login
line vty 0 4
 password cisco
 login
```

This configuration sets the enable secret to class and requires a login and password for all console, AUX port, and virtual terminal connections. The AUX port is usually a modem. The password for these connections is set to **cisco**.

Note: You can set each of the passwords to something else if you want.

Step 6

Save the open file in Notepad to a floppy disk as **start.txt**.

Select all the lines in the Notepad document and choose **Edit** > **Copy**.

Step 7

Use the Windows taskbar to return to the HyperTerminal session, and enter global configuration mode.

From the HyperTerminal Edit menu, choose **Paste to Host**.

Issue the **show run** command to see whether the configuration looks correct.

As a shortcut, you can paste the contents of the **start.txt** file to any router before getting started with a lab.

Other Useful Commands

To enhance the **start.txt** file, consider adding one of the following commands:

- **ip subnet-zero** ensures that an older IOS allows IP addresses from subnet 0.

- **ip http server** allows access to the router using a web browser. Although this configuration might not be desirable on a production router, it does enable an HTTP server for testing purposes in the lab.

- **no ip domain-lookup** prevents the router from attempting to query a Domain Name System (DNS) when you enter a word that is not recognized as a command or a host table entry. This feature saves time when you make a typo or misspell a command.

- **logging synchronous** in the **line con 0** configuration returns to a fresh line when the input is interrupted by a console logging message.

- You can use **configure terminal (config t)** in a file so that you do not have to type a command before pasting the contents of the file to the router.

Step 8

Use the Windows taskbar to return to Notepad and edit the lines so that they read as shown:

```
config t
!
enable secret class
ip subnet-zero
ip http server
no ip domain-lookup
line con 0
 logging synchronous
 password cisco
 login
 transport input none
line aux 0
```

```
password cisco
 login
line vty 0 4
password cisco
 login
!
end
copy run start
```

Save the file to the floppy disk so the work is not lost.

Select and copy all the lines, and return to the HyperTerminal session.

Because you included the **config t** command in the script, entering global configuration mode before pasting is no longer necessary.

If necessary, return to privileged EXEC mode. From the Edit menu, select **Paste to Host**.

After the paste is complete, confirm the copy operation.

Use **show run** to see whether the configuration looks correct.

Using Notepad to Assist in Editing

Understanding how to use Notepad can reduce typing and typos during editing sessions. Another major benefit is that you can do an entire router configuration in Notepad when at home or at the office and then paste it to the router console when access is available. In the next steps, you see a simple editing example.

Step 9

Configure the router with the following commands:

```
Router#config t
Router(config)#router rip
Router(config-router)#network 192.168.1.0
Router(config-router)#network 192.168.2.0
Router(config-router)#network 192.168.3.0
Router(config-router)#network 192.168.4.0
Router(config-router)#network 192.168.5.0
```

Press **Ctrl+Z**, and verify the configuration with **show run**. This code sets up Routing Information Protocol (RIP) to advertise a series of networks. However, the routing protocol is to change to Interior Gateway Routing Protocol (IGRP). With the **no router rip** command, you completely remove the RIP process. You still need to retype the **network** commands. The next steps show an alternative method.

Step 10

Issue the **show run** command and hold the output so that the **router rip** commands are displayed. Using the keyboard or mouse, select the **router rip** command and all **network** statements.

Copy the selection.

Use the taskbar to return to Notepad.

Open a new document and paste the selection onto the blank page.

Step 11

In the new document, type the word **no** and a space in front of the word **router**.

Press the **End** key, and press **Enter**.

Type **router igrp 100,** but do not press **Enter**. The result should appear as follows:

```
no router rip
router igrp 100
 network 192.168.1.0
 network 192.168.2.0
 network 192.168.3.0
 network 192.168.4.0
 network 192.168.5.0
```

Step 12

Select the results and copy them.

Use the taskbar to return to the HyperTerminal session.

While in global configuration mode, paste the results.

Use the **show run** command to verify the configuration.

Reflection

How could using copy and paste with Notepad be helpful in other editing situations?

_____

_____

Lab 1.5.2: Introductory Lab 2—Capturing HyperTerminal and Telnet Sessions

Estimated Time: 30 Minutes

Objective

This activity describes how to capture HyperTerminal and Telnet sessions.

Note: Mastering these techniques will reduce the amount of typing in later labs and while working in the field. These techniques are useful when perusing and testing on a production router while troubleshooting a problem.

Equipment Requirements

This lab requires the following equipment:

- A single router, preferably a 2600 series, and a workstation running a Windows operating system

Step 1

Log in to a router using HyperTerminal.

It is possible to capture the results of the HyperTerminal session in a text file, which you can view, edit, and print using Notepad, WordPad, or Microsoft Word.

Note: This feature captures future screens, not what is currently onscreen. Basically, it turns on a recording session.

To start a capture session, choose the menu option **Transfer > Capture Text**. The Capture Text dialog box appears, as shown in Figure 1-1.

Figure 1-1 Capture Text Dialog Box

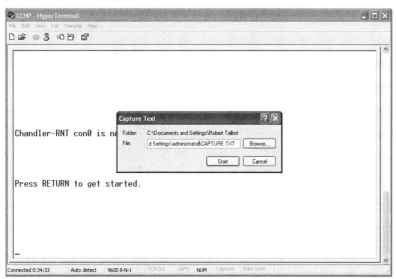

The default filename for a HyperTerminal capture is **capture.txt**, and the default location of this file is **C:\Program Files\Accessories\HyperTerminal**.

Make sure that the floppy disk is in the A: drive. When the Capture Text dialog box appears, change the File path to **A:\TestRun.txt**.

Click the **Start** button. Anything that appears onscreen after this point is copied to the file.

Step 2

Go to user privileged configuration mode. Then, issue the **show running config** command and view the entire configuration file.

From the Transfer menu, choose **Capture Text** > **Stop**.

Step 3

Using the Start menu, launch Windows Explorer. Windows Explorer might appear under Programs or Accessories, depending on which version of Windows you use.

In the left pane, select the **3½ floppy (A:)** drive. On the right side, you should see the file that you just created.

Double-click the **TestRun.txt** document icon. The result should look something like the following:

```
Router# show running configuration
Building configuration...

Current configuration:
!
version 12.0
service timestamps debug uptime
service timestamps log uptime
no service password-encryption
!
hostname Router
!
enable secret 5 $1$HD2B$6iXb.h6QEJJjtn/NnwUHO.
!
!
ip subnet-zero
no ip domain-lookup
!
interface FastEthernet0/0
no ip address
 --More--
 no ip directed-broadcast
 shutdown
```

You might see unrecognizable characters near the word **More**. Such characters appear because you press the spacebar to see the rest of the output. You can use basic word processing techniques to clean it up.

Suggestion

Consider capturing each router configuration for every lab that you do. Capture files can be useful as you review configuration features and prepare for certification exams.

Reflection

Could the capture techniques be useful if a member of the lab team misses a lab session?
Can you use capture techniques to configure an offsite lab?

_____

_____

_____

_____

_____

Lab 1.5.3: Introductory Lab 3—Access Control List Basics and Extended Ping

Estimated Time: 45 Minutes

Objective

This lab activity reviews the basics of standard and extended access lists, which are used extensively in the CCNP curriculum. You use Figure 1-2 as a sample topology in this lab.

Figure 1-2   Sample Topology for Lab 1.5.3

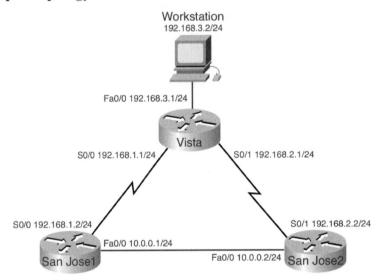

Equipment Requirements

This lab requires the following equipment:

- Three routers, preferably 2600 series, and a workstation running a Windows operating system

Scenario

The LAN users connected to the Vista router, shown in Figure 1-2, are concerned about access to their network from hosts on network 10.0.0.0. Use a standard access list to block all access to Vista's LAN from network 10.0.0.0/24.

After removing the standard access list, use an extended access control list (ACL) to block network 192.168.3.0 host access to web servers on the 10.0.0.0/24 network.

Step 1

Build and configure the network according to the diagram. Use RIP Version 1 (v1) and enable updates on all active interfaces with the appropriate **network** commands. The commands necessary to configure RIP v1 are as follows:

```
SanJose1(config)#router rip
SanJose1(config-router)#network 192.168.1.0
SanJose1(config-router)#network 10.0.0.0
Vista(config)#router rip
Vista(config-router)#network 192.168.1.0
```

```
Vista(config-router)#network 192.168.2.0
SanJose2(config)#router rip
SanJose2(config-router)#network 192.168.2.0
SanJose2(config-router)#network 10.0.0.0
```

Use the **ping** command to verify the work and test connectivity between all interfaces. After you verify connectivity, save your configurations for reuse in Labs 1-4 and 1-5.

Step 2

Check the routing table on Vista using the **show ip route** command. Vista should have all four networks in its table. Troubleshoot, if necessary.

ACL Basics

ACLs are simple but powerful tools. When you configure the access list, the router processes each statement in the list in the order in which it was created. If an individual packet meets the criteria of a statement, the router applies the permit or deny to that packet and checks no further list entries. The next packet to be checked starts again at the top of the list.

It is not possible to reorder statements, skip statements, edit statements, or delete statements from a numbered access list. With numbered access lists, any attempt to delete a single statement results in the deletion of the entire list. Named ACLs (NACLs) do allow for the deletion of individual statements.

The following concepts apply to both standard and extended access lists:

- **Two-step process.** First, you create the access list with one or more **access-list** commands while in global configuration mode. Second, the access list is applied to or referenced by other commands, such as the **access-group** command, to apply an ACL to an interface. An example is the following:

```
Vista#config t
Vista(config)#access-list 50 deny 10.0.0.0 0.0.0.255
Vista(config)#access-list 50 permit any
Vista(config)#interface fastethernet 0/0
Vista(config-if)#ip access-group 50 out
Vista(config-if)#^Z
```

- **Syntax and keywords.** The basic syntax for creating an access list entry is as follows:

```
router(config)#access-list acl-number {permit | deny}...
```

  The **permit** command allows packets matching the specified criteria to be accepted for whatever application to which the access list applies. The **deny** command discards packets matching the criteria on that line.

  Two important keywords that you can use with IP addresses and the **access list** command are **any** and **host**. The keyword **any** matches all hosts on all networks, equivalent to **0.0.0.0 255.255.255.255**. You can use the keyword **host** with an IP address to indicate a single host address. The syntax is **host** *ip-address*, such as **host 192.168.1.10**. It is treated exactly the same as **192.168.1.10 0.0.0.0**.

- **Implicit deny statement.** Every access list contains a final deny statement that matches all packets. It is called the *implicit deny*. Because the implicit deny statement is not visible in

show command output, it is often overlooked, with serious consequences. As an example, consider the following single line access list:

```
Router(config)#access-list 75 deny host 192.168.1.10
```

Access-list 75 clearly denies all traffic sourced from the host, 192.168.1.10. What might not be obvious is that all other traffic is discarded as well because the **deny any** is the final statement in any access list.

- **At least one permit statement is required.** There is no requirement that an ACL contain a **deny** statement. If nothing else, the **deny any** statement takes care of that. But if there are no **permit** statements, the effect is the same as if there were only a single **deny any** statement.

- **Wildcard mask.** In identifying IP addresses, ACLs use a wildcard mask instead of a subnet mask. Initially, they might look like the same thing, but closer observation reveals that they are very different. Remember that a binary 0 in a wildcard bitmask instructs the router to match the corresponding bit in the IP address.

- **In/out.** When deciding whether to apply an ACL to inbound or outbound traffic, always view things from the perspective of the router. Determine whether traffic is coming into the router, inbound, or leaving the router, outbound.

- **Applying ACLs.** You should apply extended ACLs as close to the source as possible, thereby conserving network resources. It is necessary to apply standard ACLs as close to the destination as possible because the standard ACL can match only at the source address of a packet.

Step 3

On the Vista router, create the following standard ACL and apply it to the LAN interface:

```
Vista#config t
Vista(config)#access-list 50 deny 10.0.0.0 0.0.0.255
Vista(config)#access-list 50 permit any
Vista(config)#interface fastethernet 0/0
Vista(config-if)#ip access-group 50 out
Vista(config-if)#^Z
```

Try pinging 192.168.3.2 from SanJose1.

The ping should be successful. This result might be unexpected because all traffic from the 10.0.0.0/8 network was blocked. The ping is successful because even though it came from SanJose1, it is not sourced from the 10.0.0.0/8 network. A **ping** or **traceroute** from a router uses the closest interface to the destination as the source address. Therefore, the **ping** is coming from the 192.168.1.0/24, SanJose1's Serial 0/0.

To test the ACL from SanJose1, use the extended **ping** command to specify a specific source interface:

```
SanJose1#ping 192.168.3.2
Sending 5, 100-byte ICMP Echos to 192.168.3.2, timeout is 2 seconds:
!!!!!
Success rate is 100 percent (5/5), round-trip min/avg/max = 4/4/4 ms
```

Step 4

To test the ACL from SanJose1, you must use the extended **ping** command to specify a source interface as follows. On SanJose1, issue the following commands:

```
SanJose1#ping 192.168.3.2
Sending 5, 100-byte ICMP Echos to 192.168.3.2, timeout is 2 seconds:
!!!!!
Success rate is 100 percent (5/5), round-trip min/avg/max = 4/4/4 ms
SanJose1#
SanJose1#ping
Protocol [ip]:
Target IP address: 192.168.3.2
Repeat count [5]:
Datagram size [100]:
Timeout in seconds [2]:
Extended commands [n]: y
Source address or interface: 10.0.0.1
Type of service [0]:
Set DF bit in IP header? [no]:
Validate reply data? [no]:
Data pattern [0xABCD]:
Loose, Strict, Record, Timestamp, Verbose[none]:
Sweep range of sizes [n]:
Type escape sequence to abort.
Sending 5, 100-byte ICMP Echos to 192.168.3.2, timeout is 2 seconds:
.....
Success rate is 0 percent (0/5)
```

Note: Remember that the extended **ping** works only in privileged EXEC mode.

Step 5

Standard ACLs are numbered 1–99. IOS Release 12.xx also allows standard lists to be numbered 1300–1699. Extended ACLs are numbered 100–199. IOS Release 12.xx allows lists to be numbered 2000–2699. You can use extended ACLs to enforce highly specific criteria for filtering packets. In this step, configure an extended ACL to block access to a web server.

Before proceeding, issue the **no access-list 50** and **no ip access-group 50 out** commands on the Vista router to remove the ACL configured previously.

Now, configure both SanJose1 and SanJose 2 to act as web servers, by using the **ip http server** command, shown as follows:

```
SanJose1(config)#ip http server
SanJose2(config)#ip http server
```

From the workstation at 192.168.3.2, use a web browser to view the web servers on both routers at 10.0.0.1 and 10.0.0.2. The web login requires that you enter the enable secret password for the router as the password.

After verifying the web connectivity between the workstation and the routers, proceed to Step 6.

Step 6

On the Vista router, enter the following commands:

```
Vista(config)#access-list 101 deny tcp 192.168.3.0 0.0.0.255 10.0.0.0
  0.0.0.255 eq www
Vista(config)#access-list 101 deny tcp 192.168.3.0 0.0.0.255 any eq ftp
Vista(config)#access-list 101 permit ip any any
```

```
Vista(config)#interface fastethernet 0/0
Vista(config-if)#ip access-group 101 in
```

From the workstation at 192.168.3.2, again attempt to view the web servers at 10.0.0.1 and 10.0.0.2. Both attempts should fail.

Note: It might be necessary to click on the browser Refresh button so that the screen display does not come from the browser's cache.

Next, browse SanJose1 at 192.168.1.2. Why is this site not blocked?

_____

Chapter 2

Modems and Asynchronous Dialup Connections

Lab 2.5.1: Configuring an Asynchronous Dialup Connection

Estimated Time: 35 Minutes

Objective

In this lab, you configure a Cisco router to support an out-of-band management EXEC session through a modem. You connect the modem to the serial interface on the router that you configure to support an asynchronous connection. You also use a workstation to remotely dial in to the router. Figure 2-1 shows the sample topology you use in this lab.

Figure 2-1   Sample Topology for Lab 2.5.1

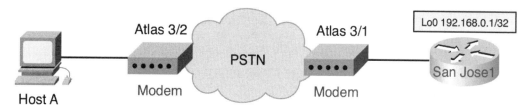

Equipment Requirements

This lab requires a host PC, two modems, one Adtran or similar device, and a router, connected as shown in Figure 2-1. This lab cannot use 2500 series routers.

Scenario

The International Travel Agency wants the serial interface on the SanJose1 core router configured to accept dialup connections. The result is that you can remotely manage the router in the event of a network failure. As the network administrator, configure the modem to allow management sessions only. You do not set up dial-on-demand routing (DDR).

Step 1

Before beginning this lab, it is recommended that you reload the router after erasing the startup configuration. Taking such a step prevents problems that might be caused by residual configurations. Build the network according to Figure 2-1, but do not configure the interface on the router. Use the Adtran Atlas 550 or similar device to simulate the Public Switched Telephone Network (PSTN). If you use the Atlas 550, you must plug the line cables from both modems into the octal FXS voice module ports of the Atlas 550, as labeled in the figure.

Note: Figure 2-1 assumes the octal FXS voice module is installed in slot 3.

Tip: Be sure to use the appropriate cable to connect the modem to the serial interface on the router. The specific cable depends upon the router model and type of physical serial interface. For example, you use different cables for a Smart Serial interface and a DB-60 serial interface.

Step 2

Configure the serial interface on SanJose1 for an asynchronous connection to assign a TTY line number to the serial interface as follows:

```
SanJose1(config)#interface s0/1
SanJose1(config-if)#physical-layer async
```

After entering these commands, issue the **show interface s0/1** command, as shown:

```
SanJose1#show interface s0/1
Serial0/1 is down, line protocol is down
  Hardware is PQUICC Serial in async mode
  MTU 1500 bytes, BW 9 Kbit, DLY 100000 usec,
     reliability 255/255, txload 1/255, rxload 1/255
  Encapsulation SLIP, loopback not set
  DTR is pulsed for 5 seconds on reset
  Last input never, output never, output hang never
  Last clearing of "show interface" counters never
  Input queue: 0/75/0 (size/max/drops); Total output drops: 0
  Queueing strategy: weighted fair
  Output queue: 0/1000/64/0 (size/max total/threshold/drops)
     Conversations  0/0/16 (active/max active/max total)
     Reserved Conversations 0/0 (allocated/max allocated)
********output omitted********
```

1.   What is the default encapsulation type for an interface in physical layer async mode?

After you configure the serial interface as asynchronous, determine the line number being used for the interface. If you are unfamiliar with the numbering scheme for this router model, you can use the **show line** command to determine the line number, as shown in the following example:

```
SanJose1#show line
   Tty Typ    Tx/Rx     A Modem  Roty AccO AccI  Uses  Noise  Overruns    Int
*    0 CTY              -   -      -    -    -     0      0      0/0        -
     2 TTY   9600/9600  -   -      -    -    -     0      0      0/0       Se0/1
    65 AUX   9600/9600  -   -      -    -    -     0      0      0/0        -
    66 VTY              -   -      -    -    -     0      0      0/0        -
    67 VTY              -   -      -    -    -     0      0      0/0        -
    68 VTY              -   -      -    -    -     0      0      0/0        -
    69 VTY              -   -      -    -    -     0      0      0/0        -
    70 VTY              -   -      -    -    -     0      0      0/0        -

Lines not in async mode -or- with no hardware support:    1 and 3 through 64.
```

The shaded portion of the sample **show line** command output shows that Serial 0/1 is TTY 2.

Use the **show line** output from the router to obtain the correct line number. Enter line configuration mode, as shown in the following example:

```
SanJose1(config)#line 2
SanJose1(config-line)#
```

The router prompt indicates that it is now in line configuration mode.

Step 3

From line configuration mode, configure the router to authenticate connections with the password **cisco**, shown as follows:

```
SanJose1(config-line)#login
SanJose1(config-line)#password cisco
```

Set the line speed and flow control type as follows:

```
SanJose1(config-line)#speed 115200
SanJose1(config-line)#flowcontrol hardware
```

Next, configure the line for both incoming and outgoing calls and allow incoming calls using all available protocols. The following commands allow reverse Telnet to the modem:

```
SanJose1(config-line)#modem inout
SanJose1(config-line)#transport input all
```

The default number of stopbits used by the asynchronous line of the router is two. Configure the line to use only one stopbit as follows:

```
SanJose1(config-line)#stopbits 1
```

Reducing the number of stopbits from two to one will improve throughput by reducing asynchronous framing overhead.

Step 4

In this step, configure a router interface for TCP/IP. The router must have an operational interface with a valid IP address to establish a reverse Telnet connection to the modem. Although you can configure a physical interface with an IP address, configure SanJose1 with a loopback interface. A loopback interface is the best way to assign an IP address to the router because loopbacks are immune to link failure. Use the following commands to configure the loopback interface:

```
SanJose1(config-line)#interface loopback0
SanJose1(config-if)#ip address 192.168.0.1 255.255.255.255
```

Notice that you use a 32-bit mask when configuring a loopback IP address. If you do not use a 32-bit mask, the router is configured as if it were connected to an entire subnet or network.

Step 5

Before establishing a Telnet session, secure virtual terminal access with the following commands:

```
SanJose1(config-if)#line vty 0 4
SanJose1(config-line)#login
SanJose1(config-line)#password cisco
SanJose1(config-line)#exit
```

Use the following command to open the reverse Telnet session to line 2:

```
SanJose1#telnet 192.168.0.1 2002
```

Note: If the router is not using line 2, change the last number to the line number appropriate to the router.

At this point, a prompt should appear for a login password. Type the password **cisco** and press the **Enter** key. This step should begin a session with the modem. Although there is no prompt, issue the following command:

```
AT
```

If the modem responds with an OK, you have established a successful reverse Telnet connection. If you do not receive an **OK** response, troubleshoot the configuration.

Step 6

View the current configuration on the modem by issuing the **AT&V** command. The following is a sample output:

```
OK
AT&V

        Option                  Selection           AT Cmd
        ---------------         ------------        --------
        Comm Standard           Bell                B
        CommandCharEcho         Enabled             E
        Speaker Volume          Medium              L
        Speaker Control         OnUntilCarrier      M
        Result Codes            Enabled             Q
        Dialer Type             Tone                T/P
        ResultCode Form         Text                V
        ExtendResultCode        Enabled             X
        DialTone Detect         Enabled             X
        BusyTone Detect         Enabled             X
        LSD Action              Standard RS232      &C
        DTR Action              Standard RS232      &D
Press any key to continue; ESC to quit.

        Option                  Selection           AT Cmd
        ---------------         ------------        --------
        V22b Guard Tone         Disabled            &G
        Flow Control            Hardware            &K
        Error Control Mode      V42,MNP,Buffer      \N
        Data Compression        V42bis/MNP5         %C
        AutoAnswerRing#         0                   S0
        AT Escape Char          43                  S2
        CarriageReturn Char     13                  S3
        Linefeed Char           10                  S4
        Backspace Char          8                   S5
        Blind Dial Pause        2 sec               S6
        NoAnswer Timeout        50 sec              S7
        "," Pause Time          2 sec               S8
Press any key to continue; ESC to quit.

        Option                  Selection           AT Cmd
        ---------------         ------------        --------
        No Carrier Disc         2000 msec           S10
        DTMF Dial Speed         95 msec             S11
        Escape GuardTime        1000 msec           S12
        Data Calling Tone       Disabled            S35
        Line Rate               33600               S37
Press any key to continue; ESC to quit.

        Stored Phone Numbers
        --------------------
         &Z0=
         &Z1=
         &Z2=
```

The modem outputs its configuration information, which is stored in NVRAM. Reset the modem to the factory defaults by entering the following command:

AT&F

After you reset the modem, issue the **AT&V** command again. The following is a sample output from the command:

```
AT&V

        Option                Selection     AT Cmd
        ---------------       ------------  --------
        Comm Standard         Bell          B
        CommandCharEcho       Enabled       E
        Speaker Volume        Medium        L
        Speaker Control       OnUntilCarrier M
        Result Codes          Enabled       Q
        Dialer Type           Tone          T/P
        ResultCode Form       Text          V
        ExtendResultCode      Enabled       X
        DialTone Detect       Enabled       X
        BusyTone Detect       Enabled       X
        LSD Action            Standard RS232 &C
        DTR Action            Standard RS232 &D
Press any key to continue; ESC to quit.

        Option                Selection     AT Cmd
        ---------------       ------------  --------
        V22b Guard Tone       Disabled      &G
        Flow Control          Hardware      &K
        Error Control Mode    V42,MNP,Buffer \N
        Data Compression      V42bis/MNP5   %C
        AutoAnswerRing#       0             S0
        AT Escape Char        43            S2
        CarriageReturn Char   13            S3
        Linefeed Char         10            S4
        Backspace Char        8             S5
        Blind Dial Pause      2 sec         S6
        NoAnswer Timeout      50 sec        S7
        "," Pause Time        2 sec         S8
Press any key to continue; ESC to quit.

        Option                Selection     AT Cmd
        ---------------       ------------  --------
        No Carrier Disc       2000 msec     S10
        DTMF Dial Speed       95 msec       S11
        Escape GuardTime      1000 msec     S12
        Data Calling Tone     Disabled      S35
        Line Rate             33600         S37
Press any key to continue; ESC to quit.

        Stored Phone Numbers
        -------------------
        &Z0=
        &Z1=
        &Z2=
```

Note: Depending on the version of firmware, the preceding output might differ.

1.   What is the Speaker Volume set to?

_____

2.   According to the output of the **AT&V** command, what **AT** command do you use to configure the speaker volume?

_____

3.   What is the AutoAnswerRing# set to?

_____

4.   What **AT** command do you use to configure the AutoAnswerRing#?

_____

5.   What is the Flow Control set to?

_____

6.   What **AT** command do you use to configure the Flow Control?

_____

Notice that you must include the ampersand (&) character, which denotes an "advanced" command, in certain **AT** commands.

Configure the modem to answer on the second ring using the following command:

`ATS0=2`

Adjust the speaker volume on the modem by using the following command:

`ATL3`

Use the appropriate command, **AT&V**, to view the current settings on the modem and verify that the configurations have taken effect.

Finally, save the configurations to NVRAM with the following command:

`AT&W`

Step 7

Now that the modem is configured, suspend the reverse Telnet session by pressing **Ctrl+Shift+6** at the same time, release, and then press **X**. This step should now return to the router prompt. From the router prompt, disconnect the reverse Telnet session to the modem as follows:

`SanJose1#disconnect`

If you do not disconnect this session, the router cannot connect using dialup.

On Host A, use the modem control panel to check that the modem is properly installed and working. Run HyperTerminal and select the modem from the Connect To window. Then, configure HyperTerminal to dial the appropriate number. If you use the Adtran Atlas 550, this number is 555-6001.

At the password prompt, enter the **cisco** password. Next, you see the SanJose1 user mode prompt. Issue the **who** command as follows:

`SanJose1>who`

```
    Line       User        Host(s)          Idle Location
    0 con 0                idle             00:26:49
*   2 tty 2                idle             00:00:00

   Interface  User        Mode             Idle Peer Address
```

1.   According to the output of this command, what TTY are you using to communicate with the router?

_____

2.   Because you cannot use this connection to route TCP/IP traffic, what is the benefit of configuring a serial interface to accept calls this way?

_____

Lab 2.5.2: Configuring an Asynchronous Dialup Connection on the AUX Port

Estimated Time: 25 Minutes

Objective

In this lab, you configure an AUX port on a Cisco router to support an out-of-band management EXEC session through a modem. You also configure the router to accept dial-in connections from a workstation. Figure 2-2 shows the sample topology you use in this lab.

Figure 2-2   Sample Topology for Lab 2.5.2

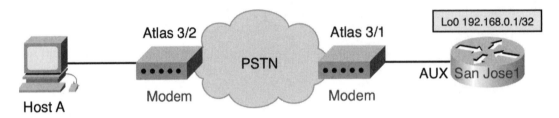

Equipment Requirements

This lab requires a host PC, two modems, one Adtran or similar device, and a router, connected as shown in Figure 2-2. This lab cannot use 2500 series routers.

Scenario

The International Travel Agency configured the SanJose1 core router to accept dialup connections on its AUX port. As a result, you can manage it remotely in the event of a network failure. As the network administrator, configure the modem to allow management sessions only. You do not set up DDR.

Step 1

Before beginning this lab, it is recommended that you reload each router after erasing its startup configuration. Taking this step prevents problems that might be caused by residual configurations. Build the network according to Figure 2-2. Use the Adtran Atlas 550 or similar device to simulate the PSTN. If you use the Atlas 550, be sure that you plug the line cables from both modems into the octal FXS voice module ports of the Atlas 550, as labeled in the figure.

Use a rollover cable and DCE modem adapter to connect the external modem to the AUX port on the router.

Step 2

Configure the AUX port on SanJose1 for an asynchronous connection that will use authentication as follows:

```
SanJose1(config)#line aux 0
SanJose1(config-line)#login
SanJose1(config-line)#password cisco
```

Set the line speed, flow control type, and number of stopbits as follows:

```
SanJose1(config-line)#speed 115200
SanJose1(config-line)#flowcontrol hardware
SanJose1(config-line)#stopbits 1
```

Notice that the maximum speed supported by the AUX port varies depending on the model router. On the 2600 and 3600 series routers, 115,200 bits per second (bps) is the maximum, whereas other platforms might only support up to 38,400 bps. Typically, you should set the modem speed to the maximum bitrate supported by both the router and the modem. Next, configure the line for both incoming and outgoing calls. Allow incoming calls using all available protocols and set an enable secret password. Use the following configurations to perform this task:

```
SanJose1(config-line)#modem inout
SanJose1(config-line)#transport input all
SanJose1(config-line)#exit
SanJose1(config)#enable secret class
SanJose1(config)#exit
```

Step 3

On SanJose1, issue the **show line** command at the router prompt. A sample output follows:

```
SanJose1#show line
   Tty Typ     Tx/Rx      A Modem  Roty AccO AccI   Uses  Noise  Overruns  Int
*    0 CTY                - -      -    -    -       1     0      0/0       -
*   65 AUX 115200/115200- inout    -    -    -       1     1      24/0      -
    66 VTY                - -      -    -    -       0     0      0/0       -
    67 VTY                - -      -    -    -       0     0      0/0       -
    68 VTY                - -      -    -    -       0     0      0/0       -
    69 VTY                - -      -    -    -       0     0      0/0       -
    70 VTY                - -      -    -    -       0     0      0/0       -

Line(s) not in async mode -or- with no hardware support: 1-64
```

1. According to the output of this command, what is the line number for the AUX port on the router?

_____

Note: The line number can vary depending on the router platform.

At this point, have the router automatically configure the modem without establishing a reverse Telnet connection. Issue the **debug confmodem** command to monitor the autoconfiguration process. Now, refer to the displayed AUX line number and configure the modem to use the Cisco IOS autoconfiguration feature.

Enter the following commands:

```
SanJose1#debug confmodem
SanJose1#configure terminal
SanJose1(config)#line 65
SanJose1(config-line)#modem autoconfigure discovery
```

After you type the **modem autoconfigure discovery** command, you see the debug output as the router queries and configures the modem. The entire process can take 30 seconds or more. The output should look similar to the following:

```
00:37:32: TTY65: detection speed (115200) response ---OK---
00:37:38: TTY65: Modem type is default
00:37:38: TTY65: Modem command:  --AT&F&C1&D2S0=1H0--
00:37:38: TTY65: Modem configuration succeeded
00:37:38: TTY65: Detected modem speed 115200
00:37:38: TTY65: Done with modem configuration
```

Notice that the Cisco IOS modem discovery feature is unlikely to provide an optimal modem configuration. Therefore, whenever possible, configure the modem manually using reverse Telnet or a specific modem configuration script.

Even though you used the modem autoconfiguration feature, you might need to establish a reverse Telnet session to the modem through the AUX port.

2.   What port number would you use to Telnet to connect to the modem on the AUX port?

Step 4

At the console of SanJose1, enter the following commands to enable a Telnet session with password authentication and an active interface:

```
SanJose1(config)#line vty 0 4
SanJose1(config-line)#login
SanJose1(config-line)#password cisco
SanJose1(config-line)#interface loopback 0
SanJose1(config-if)#ip address 192.168.0.1 255.255.255.255
```

1.   Why should you assign a password to the virtual terminals?

---

2.   Why did you need to assign an IP address to a loopback interface?

---

3.   Why do you use a 32-bit mask with the loopback address?

To simplify the reverse Telnet connection, create a static host entry called **auxmodem** with the **ip host** command. Use the port number 2000+, the TTY #, and the loopback interface IP address. For example, on a Cisco 2600 series router, the TTY number of the AUX port is 65. Therefore, the port number is 2065. Enter the following command to create a host table mapping that includes both the IP address and the reverse Telnet port number:

```
SanJose1(config)#ip host auxmodem 2065 192.168.0.1
```

After you configure the host table mapping, you need type only the host name to start a Telnet session. Enter the following host name at the prompt:

```
SanJose1#auxmodem
```

Typing this host name should open a reverse Telnet session with the modem. Issue the **AT&V** command to verify communication to the modem. Troubleshoot as necessary.

Now that the modem is configured, suspend the reverse Telnet session by pressing **Ctrl+Shift+6** at the same time, release, and press **X**. This step should return you to the router prompt. From the router prompt, disconnect the reverse Telnet session to the modem as follows:

```
SanJose1#disconnect
```

Step 5

On Host A, use the modem control panel to check that the modem is properly installed and working. Run HyperTerminal and select the modem in the Connect To window. Then, use HyperTerminal to dial the appropriate number. If you use the Adtran Atlas 550, this number is 555-6001.

If Host A successfully connects to SanJose1, you see a password prompt. At the password prompt, enter the password **class** to access the router. Troubleshoot as necessary.

Lab 2.5.3: Configuring an Asynchronous Dialup PPP

Estimated Time: 25 Minutes

Objective

In this lab, you configure two Cisco routers to connect to each other asynchronously using PPP. You also configure two Cisco routers to support in-band user sessions through modems connected to the SanJose1 and Capetown serial interfaces. You configure the asynchronous connections to support PPP encapsulation and DDR.

Configure each router with their respective host name and Fast Ethernet IP addresses. Configure each workstation with the correct IP address and default gateway.

Figure 2-3 shows the sample topology for this lab.

Figure 2-3   Sample Topology for Lab 2.5.3

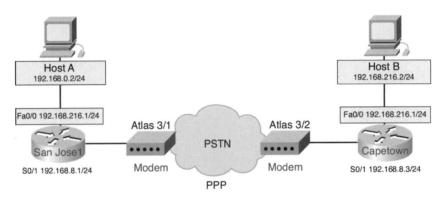

Equipment Requirements

This lab requires a host PC, two modems, one Adtran or similar device, and two routers, connected as shown in Figure 2-3. This lab cannot use 2500 series routers.

Scenario

The International Travel Agency wants to allow Capetown to access the router of the company headquarters, SanJose1. Capetown needs only occasional access to company e-mail. As the network administrator, configure a dialup PPP connection between the two sites. When you are finished, Capetown must be able to establish a DDR connection to SanJose1. Verify this configuration by pinging between the Capetown Host B and the SanJose1 Host A.

Step 1

Before beginning this lab, it is recommended that you reload each router after erasing its startup configuration. Taking this step prevents problems that might be caused by residual configurations. Build and configure the network according to Figure 2-3, but do not configure the serial interfaces on either router yet. Use the Adtran Atlas 550 or similar device to simulate the PSTN. If you use the Atlas 550, be sure that you plug the line cables from both modems into the octal FXS voice module ports of the Atlas 550, as labeled in the figure. Also, be sure to configure both workstations with the correct IP address and default gateway, router Fa0/0 IP address.

Step 2

Configure the serial interface on Capetown for an asynchronous connection as follows:

```
Capetown(config)#interface serial 0/1
Capetown(config-if)#physical-layer async
Capetown(config-if)#ip address 192.168.8.3 255.255.255.0
Capetown(config-if)#encapsulation ppp
Capetown(config-if)#async mode dedicated
```

Notice that the serial interface uses PPP encapsulation.

1.   What is the default encapsulation type for a serial interface when in physical layer async mode?

The **async mode dedicated** command puts the interface in dedicated asynchronous network mode. In this mode, the interface only uses the specified encapsulation, which is PPP in this case. An EXEC prompt does not appear, and the router is not available for normal interactive use.

Because you are configuring a low-bandwidth dialup connection, turn off Cisco Discovery Protocol (CDP) updates to reduce bandwidth usage as follows:

```
Capetown(config-if)#no cdp enable
```

Enter additional commands, as follows, so that Capetown can dial SanJose1.

The **dialer in-band** command specifies that the interface supports DDR:

```
Capetown(config-if)#dialer in-band
```

The **dialer idle-timeout** command specifies the number of seconds the router allows the connection to remain idle before disconnecting. The default is 120 seconds:

```
Capetown(config-if)#dialer idle-timeout 300
```

The `dialer` **wait-for-carrier-time** command specifies the length of time the interface waits for a carrier when trying to establish a connection. The default wait time is 30 seconds. The routers in this lab use a chat script to initialize the modem and cause it to dial:

```
Capetown(config-if)#dialer wait-for-carrier-time 60
```

Note: You configure a chat script later in this step. On asynchronous interfaces, the **dialer wait-for-carrier-time** command essentially sets the total time allowed for the chat script to run.

You use the **dialer hold-queue** command to allow outgoing packets to queue until a modem connection is established. If you do not configure a hold queue, packets are dropped during the time required to establish a connection. The **50** in this command specifies 50 packets:

```
Capetown(config-if)#dialer hold-queue 50
```

The **dialer-group** command controls access by configuring an interface to belong to a specific dialing group. In Step 3, you use the **dialer-list** command to configure interesting traffic that will trigger DDR for interfaces belonging to group 1:

```
Capetown(config-if)#dialer-group 1
```

This **dialer map** command creates mapping between an IP address and the phone number that you should dial to reach that address. It also tells the router to use the appropriate chat script. DDR uses chat scripts to issue commands to dial a modem and log on to remote systems.

```
Capetown(config-if)#dialer map ip 192.168.8.1 name SanJose1 modem-script
  hayes56k broadcast 5556001
```

Return to the global configuration mode to define the chat script. Use the following command with Hayes 56 K Accura modems:

```
Capetown(config)#chat-script hayes56k ABORT ERROR "" "AT Z" OK "ATDT \T"
  TIMEOUT 30 CONNECT \c
```

Step 3

After you configure the serial interface and chat script for asynchronous PPP, configure the following line parameters:

```
Capetown(config)#line 2
Capetown(config-line)#speed 115200
Capetown(config-line)#flowcontrol hardware
Capetown(config-line)#modem inout
Capetown(config-line)#transport input all
Capetown(config-line)#stopbits 1
```

1.   What is the default number of stopbits on a line?

_____

_____

Step 4

On Capetown, define interesting traffic to establish a dial-up connection for IP traffic as follows:

```
Capetown(config)#dialer-list 1 protocol ip permit
```

Because this dialer list is number 1, it is linked to dialer group 1. The **dialer-list** command specifies the traffic that is to be permitted on interfaces that belong to the corresponding dialer group.

For Capetown to route traffic through the Serial 0/1 interface, configure this default route to the central site as follows:

```
Capetown(config)#ip route 0.0.0.0 0.0.0.0 192.168.8.1
```

This step completes the Capetown router configuration.

Step 5

Configure the company headquarters router, SanJose1. Enter the following commands:

```
SanJose1(config)#interface s0/1
SanJose1(config-if)#physical-layer async
SanJose1(config-if)#ip address 192.168.8.1 255.255.255.0
SanJose1(config-if)#encapsulation ppp
SanJose1(config-if)#async mode dedicated
SanJose1(config-if)#no cdp enable
SanJose1(config)#line 2
SanJose1(config-line)#speed 115200
SanJose1(config-line)#flowcontrol hardware
SanJose1(config-line)#modem inout
```

```
SanJose1(config-line)#transport input all
SanJose1(config-line)#stopbits 1
SanJose1(config-line)#modem autoconfigure discovery
SanJose1(config)#ip route 192.168.216.0 255.255.255.0 192.168.8.3
```

Step 6

Write the SanJose1 and Capetown configurations to NVRAM and reload the routers. Power cycle the modem and the Adtran Atlas 550. Taking this step helps avoid potential problems caused by residual configurations.

Step 7

From the Capetown Host B, ping the SanJose1 Host A (192.168.0.2). The first set of pings fails because the modems must perform the handshaking sequence to establish a connection (approximately 20 seconds). Once a connection is established, issue the **ping** command a second or third time. Eventually, the ping should be successful, which means the Capetown Host B has dialed the SanJose1 Host A and the configuration is working. Troubleshoot as necessary.

After you verify successful pings, issue the **show dialer** command on Capetown. The following is a sample output:

```
Capetown#show dialer

Serial0/1 - dialer type = IN-BAND ASYNC NO-PARITY
Idle timer (300 secs), Fast idle timer (20 secs)
Wait for carrier (60 secs), Re-enable (15 secs)
Dialer state is data link layer up
Dial reason: ip (s=192.168.216.2, d=192.168.0.2)
Time until disconnect 217 secs
Connected to 5556001
Dial String      Successes    Failures    Last DNIS    Last status
5556001                  1           0     00:04:19     successful
```

1.   What is the dialer type of S0/1?

_____

_____

2.   What is the dialer state?

_____

_____

3.   What is the dial reason?

_____

_____

4.   How much longer will this connection remain up if it is idle?

_____

_____

Chapter 3

PPP Overview

Lab 3.7.1: Configuring PPP Interactive Mode

Estimated Time: 30 Minutes

Objective

In this lab, you configure a Cisco router to connect asynchronously to a modem and use a
workstation, Host A, to remotely dial into the router. You also configure PPP interactive mode so
that the user on Host A can select between a PPP session and a router management EXEC
session when using HyperTerminal for dialing out. Figure 3-1 shows the sample topology for
this lab.

Figure 3-1   Sample Topology for Lab 3.7.1

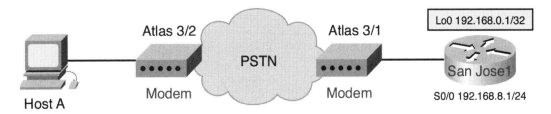

Equipment Requirements

This lab requires a host PC, two modems, one Adtran or similar device, and two routers,
connected as shown in Figure 3-1. This lab cannot use 2500 series routers.

Scenario

The International Travel Agency wants dialup access configured to the central router SanJose1.
It wants access set up so that the remote user at Host A can dial up the router for either an EXEC
management session on the router or a PPP connection to the corporate LAN. This configuration
will allow the dialup user to choose between configuring the router remotely and accessing the
central site network. Because the user can choose to access International Travel Agency's
TCP/IP-based network, this configuration must account for assigning an IP address to Host A.

Step 1

Before beginning this lab, it is recommended that you reload the router after erasing its startup
configuration. Taking this step prevents problems that might be caused by residual
configurations. Build and configure the network according to the diagram, but do not configure
SanJose1's serial interface yet. Configure SanJose1 with the appropriate host name and
Loopback 0 IP address shown. Use the Adtran Atlas 550, or similar device, to simulate the
Public Switched Telephone Network (PSTN). If you use the Atlas 550, be sure that you plug the
line cables from both modems into the octal FXS voice module ports of the Atlas 550, as labeled
in Figure 3-1.

Step 2

Configure the serial interface on SanJose1 for an asynchronous connection, as follows:

```
SanJose1(config)#interface s0/0
SanJose1(config-if)#physical-layer async
SanJose1(config-if)#ip address 192.168.8.1 255.255.255.0
SanJose1(config-if)#async mode interactive
SanJose1(config-if)#peer default ip address 192.168.8.5
```

The **async mode interactive** command allows the remote user to select between a PPP session and an EXEC session with the router. The **peer default ip address** command configures the router to assign an IP address to the dial-in host. An IP address is required for the remote host to access the International Travel Agency corporate network.

Because you use Telnet and reverse Telnet in this exercise, configure the virtual terminals on SanJose1 with the following commands:

```
SanJose1(config)#line vty 0 4
SanJose1(config-line)#login
SanJose1(config-line)#password cisco
```

Step 3

Configure the appropriate line so that it can communicate with the modem as follows:

```
SanJose1(config)#line 2
SanJose1(config-line)#login
SanJose1(config-line)#password cisco
SanJose1(config-line)#speed 115200
SanJose1(config-line)#flowcontrol hardware
SanJose1(config-line)#modem inout
SanJose1(config-line)#transport input all
SanJose1(config-line)#stopbits 1
```

Note: Line 2 is used here as an example; use **show line** to verify the actual number for the router.

For this scenario, also configure the following line to select PPP automatically:

```
SanJose1(config-line)#autoselect ppp
```

The **autoselect** command configures the Cisco IOS software to identify the type of connection being requested. You use this command on lines making different types of connections.

Finally, reverse Telnet to the modem, restore the factory default settings (**AT&F**) on the modem, and configure the modem to answer on the second ring (**ATS0=2**), as follows:

```
SanJose1#telnet 192.168.0.1 200x
!x is the Line number of S0/0 Async
Password: cisco
AT
OK
AT&F
ATS0=2
```

1.   What port number do you use to establish a reverse Telnet session with the modem?

_____

_____

Now that the modem is configured, suspend the reverse Telnet session by pressing **Ctrl+Shift+6** at the same time, release, and press **X**. From the router prompt, disconnect the reverse Telnet session to the modem as follows:

```
SanJose1#disconnect
```

Step 4

In this step, verify that SanJose1 is accepting dialup PPP connections from Host A.

Change the TCP/IP properties of the network card to obtain an IP address automatically.

Next, configure dialup networking (DUN) on Host A. The exact configuration steps for DUN vary depending on the operating system used by Host A. If you use Windows 9x/NT/2000/Me/XP, open the Dialup Networking folder and click the **Make New Connection** icon. In Windows 2000, this folder is called Network and Dialup Connections. In Windows XP, select the Control Panel, select Network Connections, and select Add New Connection. If you use the standard Adtran Atlas configuration, configure the connection to dial 555-6001 (port 1). Because you have not configured PPP authentication, no username or password for this connection is required.

After you name and complete the DUN configuration, double-click the connection icon and establish a dialup connection with SanJose1. If the connection fails, troubleshoot as necessary.

Once you establish the connection, check the IP address of Host A. Remember that this address is bound to the dialup adapter, not to the network interface card (NIC).

1.   What IP address is assigned to the dialup adapter?

_____

_____

Verify that Host A has TCP/IP connectivity to the corporate network by pinging the loopback interface on SanJose1, 192.168.0.1. If Host A does not receive a reply, troubleshoot as necessary.

From Host A, Telnet to SanJose1 at 192.168.8.1 and enter the appropriate password. On SanJose1, issue the **show interface s0/0** command.

The following is a partial sample output displayed on the workstation:

```
SanJose1#show interface s0/0
Serial0/0 is up, line protocol is up
  Hardware is PQUICC Serial in async mode (TTY2)
  Internet address is 192.168.8.1/24
  MTU 1500 bytes, BW 115 Kbit, DLY 100000 usec,
     reliability 255/255, txload 1/255, rxload 1/255
  Encapsulation PPP, loopback not set
  Keepalive not set
*******output omitted*******
```

2.   According to the output of the **show interface** command, what is the encapsulation set to?

_____

_____

Now that you verified TCP/IP connectivity, exit the Telnet session and disconnect the dialup link.

Step 5

Verify that SanJose1 is accepting dialup management (EXEC) sessions from Host A. Right-click the connection icon in the Dialup Networking window and select **Properties**. If you use Windows 95/98, click the **Configure** button on the **General** tab. This step opens the modem configuration window. In this window, select the **Options** tab and check the box for **Bring up terminal window after dialing**. If you use Windows NT/2000/XP, check the **Show terminal window** box on the **Security** tab. Finally, if you use Windows Me, click the Scripting tab and uncheck the **Start terminal screen minimized** box.

Now, establish the dialup connection, as in Step 4. When the router answers the call, a terminal window should appear. Press the **Enter** key to trigger the router password prompt and then enter the appropriate password.

While still connected, issue the **show interface s0/0** command on SanJose1.

1. According to the output of the **show interface** command, what is the line encapsulation set to?

    _____

    _____

2. Notice that the interface is not in an up-and-up state even though a connection is established. Why?

    _____

    _____

3. Has the dialup adapter on Host A been assigned an IP address?

    _____

    _____

Finally, because SanJose1 is using asynchronous interactive mode, begin a PPP session with the router by entering the appropriate command while in the management session. In the dialup terminal window, type the following command:

```
SanJose1>ppp
```

Strings of character output appear, representing PPP frames. In Windows 9x/Me, click the **Continue** button at the bottom of the Dialup Networking terminal window. Otherwise, click the **Done** button. After a few seconds, check the IP address of Host A. The dialup adapter should now have the address 192.168.8.5.

Verify that there is TCP/IP connectivity by Telnetting from Host A to SanJose1 through 192.168.8.1.

Lab 3.7.2: Configuring PPP Options—Authentication and Compression

Estimated Time: 30 Minutes

Objective

In this lab, you configure a Cisco router to accept PPP dialup connections over a PSTN cloud. The call originates from a workstation using key PPP options: authentication and compression. You use the sample topology shown in Figure 3-2 in this lab.

Figure 3-2   Sample Topology for Lab 3.7.2

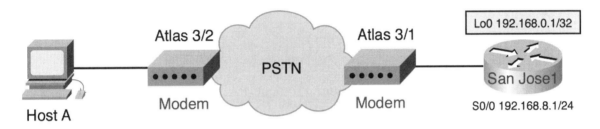

Equipment Requirements

This lab requires a host PC, two modems, one Adtran or similar device, and two routers, connected as shown in Figure 3-2. This lab cannot use 2500 series routers.

Scenario

The International Travel Agency wants dialup access configured to the central router SanJose1 using PPP. To secure dialup access, you must configure authentication. Also, you must configure compression to maximize the amount of data that can be transferred across the link.

Step 1

Before beginning this lab, it is recommended that you reload the router after erasing its startup configuration. Taking this step prevents problems that might be caused by residual configurations. Build and configure the network according to Figure 3-2, but do not configure SanJose1's serial interface yet. Configure SanJose1 with the appropriate host name and Loopback 0 IP address shown. Use the Adtran Atlas 550, or similar device, to simulate the PSTN. If you use the Atlas 550, be sure that you plug the line cables from both modems into the respective octal FXS voice module ports of the Atlas 550, as labeled in Figure 3-2.

Step 2

Configure the serial interface on SanJose1 for an asynchronous connection as follows:

```
SanJose1(config)#interface s0/0

SanJose1(config-if)#physical-layer async
SanJose1(config-if)#async mode dedicated
SanJose1(config-if)#ip address 192.168.8.1 255.255.255.0
SanJose1(config-if)#peer default ip address 192.168.8.5
```

Remember, you use the **peer default ip address** command to automatically assign the dialup host an IP address. Configure the line as follows:

```
SanJose1(config)#line 2
SanJose1(config-line)#login
SanJose1(config-line)#password cisco
SanJose1(config-line)#speed 115200
SanJose1(config-line)#flowcontrol hardware
SanJose1(config-line)#modem inout
SanJose1(config-line)#transport input all
SanJose1(config-line)#stopbits 1
```

Because you use Telnet and reverse Telnet during this exercise, configure the virtual terminals as follows:

```
SanJose1(config-line)#line vty 0 4
SanJose1(config-line)#login
SanJose1(config-line)#password cisco
```

Step 3

Configure PPP to use Password Authentication Protocol (PAP) authentication using the following commands:

```
SanJose1(config-line)#interface s0/0
SanJose1(config-if)#encapsulation ppp
SanJose1(config-if)#ppp authentication pap
SanJose1(config-if)#exit
SanJose1(config)#username hosta password itsasecret
```

Recall that PPP supports two different authentication protocols, PAP and Challenge Handshake Authentication Protocol (CHAP).

1.   Which protocol, PAP or CHAP, is considered the most secure? Why?

_____

_____

When using PPP authentication, the router checks received username and password combinations against a database. In this exercise, the username and password database is stored locally on the router. You use the **username** *name* **password** *password* command to enter this local authentication information.

Step 4

Configure PPP to use compression, using the following commands:

```
SanJose1(config)#interface s0/0
SanJose1(config-if)#compress stac
```

The **compress stac** command specifies the compression algorithm to use with PPP. You must configure both link partners to use the same compression algorithm. In this case, you configure PPP to use the stacker algorithm. It is sometimes called the Lempel-Ziv algorithm, or LZS. Stacker is CPU-intensive.

1.   What other methods of PPP compression are available?

_____

_____

You can also compress the headers of the TCP/IP packets to reduce their size, thereby increasing performance. Header compression is particularly useful on networks with a large percentage of small packets, such as those supporting many Telnet connections. This feature compresses only the TCP header. Therefore, it has no effect on User Datagram Protocol (UDP) packets or other protocol headers. Enable TCP header compression with the following command:

```
SanJose1(config-if)#ip tcp header-compression
```

Note: TCP header compression is often referred to as Van Jacobsen (VJ) compression.

Step 5

Reverse Telnet to the modem. Restore the factory default settings (**AT&F**) on the modem, configure the modem to answer on the second ring (**ATS0=2**), and then disconnect the session.

Note: Refer to Lab 3.7.1 for the procedure, if necessary.

At this point, you might need to reboot all the lab equipment to prevent potential problems with residual configurations. Save the SanJose1 configuration to NVRAM and reload the router. Power cycle the modem and the Adtran Atlas 550.

Step 6

Before configuring Host A DUN, enable PPP **debug** on SanJose1's console using the following command:

```
SanJose1#debug ppp negotiation
```

After enabling **debug**, configure DUN on Host A to dial SanJose1. If you use the standard Adtran Atlas 550 configuration, configure DUN to dial 555-6001. Use the username **hosta** and password **itsasecret**.

Be sure this connection is not configured to bring up a terminal window. From Host A, dial SanJose1. If the connection attempt fails, troubleshoot as necessary. You might need to repeat Step 5. After the connection is successful, examine the **debug** output. The output from SanJose1 should include the following:

```
********output omitted********
Se0/0 LCP: State is Open
Se0/0 PPP: Phase is AUTHENTICATING, by this end
Se0/0 PAP: I AUTH-REQ id 1 len 16 from "hosta"
Se0/0 PAP: Authenticating peer hosta
Se0/0 PAP: O AUTH-ACK id 1 len 5
Se0/0 PPP: Phase is UP
Se0/0 IPCP: O CONFREQ [Closed] id 8 len 16
Se0/0 IPCP: CompressType VJ 15 slots (0x0206002D0F00)
Se0/0 IPCP: Address 192.168.8.1 (0x03060A010101)
Se0/0 CCP: O CONFREQ [Closed] id 4 len 10
Se0/0 CCP: LZSDCP history 1 check mode SEQ process UNCOMPRESSED
(0x170600010201)
********output omitted********
```

1.   According to the **debug** output, who is the authenticating peer?

_____

_____

2. During the **AUTHENTICATING** phase, does the **debug** indicate the authentication protocol used?

_____

_____

3. What does **CompressType VJ** refer to?

_____

_____

4. What does **LZSDCP** refer to?

_____

_____

5. According to the **debug** output on SanJose1, during which PPP phase or phases are link control protocol (LCP) frames exchanged?

_____

_____

6. According to the **debug** output on SanJose1, which kinds of NCPs were exchanged between Host A and SanJose1?

_____

_____

While Host A is still connected to SanJose1, issue the **show compress** command. If you lose the connection from Host A to SanJose1, reconnect. A sample output follows:

```
SanJose1#show compress
 Serial0/0
     Software compression enabled
     uncompressed bytes xmt/rcv 0/2357
     ********output omitted********
       Additional Stacker Stats:
       Transmit bytes:  Uncompressed = 0 Compressed = 0
       Received bytes:  Compressed = 564 Uncompressed = 0
```

7. According to the output of this command, is the compression method hardware- or software-based?

_____

Disconnect the dialup session and redial using the wrong password. Leave the PPP **debug** running on SanJose1. The connection should fail.

8. What indications about why the connection failed are included in the **debug** output authenticating phase?

_____

Lab 3.7.3: Configuring PPP Callback

Estimated Time: 30 Minutes

Objective

In this lab, you configure a Cisco router for PPP callback over an asynchronous connection. You use the sample topology shown in Figure 3-3.

Figure 3-3   Sample Topology for Lab 3.7.3

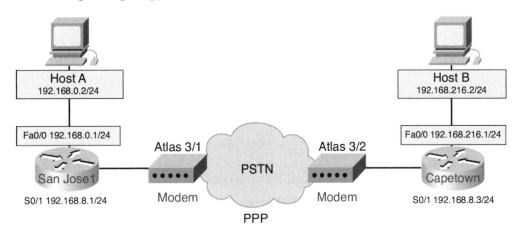

Equipment Requirement

This lab requires a host PC, two modems, one Adtran or similar device, and two routers, connected as shown in Figure 3-3. This lab cannot use 2500 series routers.

Scenario

The International Travel Agency has been incurring excessive toll charges whenever remote sites connect to the central site via a dialup connection. To reduce toll charges, International Travel Agency has secured lower call rates for calls initiated from the central site. Configure PPP callback between remote sites and the central site so that whenever a remote router calls the central router, the central router hangs up and calls the remote site back to take advantage of the lower call rates.

Step 1

Before beginning this lab, you should reload the routers after erasing their startup configuration. This step prevents problems that might be caused by residual configurations. Build and configure the network according to Figure 3-3, but do not configure the serial interfaces on either router yet. Use the Adtran Atlas 550 or similar device to simulate the PSTN. If you use the Atlas 550, be sure that you plug the line cables from both modems into the octal FXS voice module ports of the Atlas 550, as labeled in Figure 3-3. Configure each router with its respective host name and Fast Ethernet IP addresses. Finally, configure each workstation with the correct IP address and default gateway.

Step 2

Configure the serial interfaces on both routers for asynchronous connections. Be sure that you have set the correct IP addresses for each router. The following is an example of the commands for SanJose1:

```
SanJose1(config)#interface s0/1
SanJose1(config-if)#physical-layer async
SanJose1(config-if)#async mode dedicated
SanJose1(config-if)#ip address 192.168.8.1 255.255.255.0
```

Configure the following line parameters for both routers. The following is an example of the commands for SanJose1:

```
SanJose1(config)#line 2
SanJose1(config-line)#login
SanJose1(config-line)#password cisco
SanJose1(config-line)#speed 115200
SanJose1(config-line)#flowcontrol hardware
SanJose1(config-line)#modem inout
SanJose1(config-line)#transport input all
SanJose1(config-line)#stopbits 1
```

Configure the virtual terminals on both routers with passwords.

Next, reverse Telnet to both modems, restore their factory default settings, and configure the modems to answer on the second ring.

Note: Refer to Lab 3.7.1 for the procedure, if necessary.

Step 3

Configure both routers to use their modems to initiate dialup connections. On both routers, enter the appropriate **dialer** commands. The following are sample commands for SanJose1:

```
SanJose1(config)#interface serial 0/1
SanJose1(config-if)#no cdp enable
SanJose1(config-if)#dialer in-band
SanJose1(config-if)#dialer idle-timeout 300
SanJose1(config-if)#dialer wait-for-carrier-time 60
SanJose1(config-if)#dialer hold-queue 50
SanJose1(config-if)#dialer-group 1
SanJose1(config)#chat-script hayes56k ABORT ERROR "" "AT Z" OK "ATDT \T"
   TIMEOUT 30 CONNECT \c
SanJose1(config)#dialer-list 1 protocol ip permit
```

After you enter the commands on both routers, configure the dialer map on Capetown as follows:

```
Capetown(config)#interface s0/1
Capetown(config-if)#dialer map ip 192.168.8.1 name SanJose1 modem-script
   hayes56k broadcast 5556001
```

This command maps the IP address of SanJose1 to its phone number. It also specifies that the chat-script should be used to initialize the modem. Because SanJose1 is the callback server, its dialer map configuration requires additional keywords. You enter SanJose1's dialer map configuration in the next step.

Step 4

Configure SanJose1's serial interface to act as a PPP callback server. First, use the following to configure PPP for PAP authentication:

```
SanJose1(config)interface s0/1
SanJose1(config-if)#encapsulation ppp
SanJose1(config-if)#ppp authentication pap
SanJose1(config-if)#ppp pap sent-username SanJose1 password alpha
```

The **ppp pap sent-username** command configures SanJose1 to send the specified username and password combination if prompted during the PPP authentication phase.

Next, enter the PPP commands required to configure SanJose1 as a PPP callback server, as shown in the following:

```
SanJose1(config-if)#ppp callback accept
SanJose1(config-if)#dialer callback-secure
SanJose1(config-if)#exit
SanJose1(config)#username Capetown password bravo
```

The **ppp callback accept** command configures SanJose1 to accept callback requests from clients. The **dialer callback-secure** command affects those users who are not authorized to receive a callback with the **dialer callback-server** command. If the username is not authorized for callback, the call is disconnected. Next, configure authorization for callback service on SanJose1 as follows:

```
SanJose1(config)#map-class dialer dialback
SanJose1(config-map-class)#dialer callback-server username
SanJose1(config-map-class)#exit
SanJose1(config)#interface s0/1
SanJose1(config-if)#dialer map ip 192.168.8.3 name Capetown class dialback
  modem-script hayes56k broadcast 5556002
```

Step 5

Configure Capetown for PPP with PAP authentication and callback request as follows, using the **ppp callback request** command:

```
Capetown(config)#interface s0/1
Capetown(config-if)#encapsulation ppp
Capetown(config-if)#ppp authentication pap
Capetown(config-if)#ppp pap sent-username Capetown password bravo
Capetown(config-if)#ppp callback request
Capetown(config-if)#exit
Capetown(config)#username SanJose1 password alpha
```

Step 6

Set up static routes on both routers. For SanJose1, configure a static route to the Capetown LAN as follows:

```
SanJose1(config)#ip route 192.168.216.0 255.255.255.0 192.168.8.3
```

On Capetown, configure a default route to the central router as follows:

```
Capetown(config)#ip route 0.0.0.0 0.0.0.0 192.168.8.1
```

Step 7

At this point, reboot all the lab equipment to prevent potential problems with residual configurations. Save the SanJose1 and Capetown configurations to NVRAM and reload the routers. Power cycle the modems and Adtran Atlas 550.

After all the lab equipment reboots, enable debug on SanJose1's console as follows:

```
SanJose1#debug dialer
```

The **debug dialer** command outputs dialup related information to the console. Now, bring up the asynchronous connection by pinging from Host B to Host A (192.168.0.2).

1.   Which of the routing table entries on Capetown are used to route the ping packet from Host B to 192.168.0.2?

_____

_____

2.   What is the next-hop IP address mapped to that route?

_____

_____

3.   What is the phone number mapped to that address in the Capetown router configuration?

_____

_____

Capetown should call SanJose1, SanJose1 should disconnect the call, and then SanJose1 should call back Capetown. Troubleshoot as necessary. The **debug dialer** output should reflect this process, as shown in the following example:

```
SanJose1#
01:07:06: %LINK-3-UPDOWN: Interface Serial0/1, changed state to up

Dialer statechange to up Serial0/1
01:07:06: Serial0/1 DDR: Dialer received incoming call from <unknown>
01:07:08: Serial0/1 DDR: PPP callback Callback server starting to Capetown
  5556002
01:07:08: Serial0/1 DDR: disconnecting call
01:07:10: %LINK-5-CHANGED: Interface Serial0/1, changed state to reset
01:07:15: %LINK-3-UPDOWN: Interface Serial0/1, changed state to down
01:07:30: Serial0/1 DDR: re-enable timeout
01:07:30: DDR: callback triggered by dialer_timers
01:07:30: Serial0/1 DDR: beginning callback to Capetown 5556002
01:07:30: Serial0/1 DDR: Attempting to dial 5556002
01:07:30: CHAT2: Attempting async line dialer script
01:07:30: CHAT2: Dialing using Modem script: hayes56k & System script: none
01:07:30: DDR: Freeing callback to Capetown 5556002
01:07:30: CHAT2: process started
01:07:30: CHAT2: Asserting DTR
01:07:30: CHAT2: Chat script hayes56k started
01:07:58: CHAT2: Chat script hayes56k finished, status = Success
01:08:00: %LINK-3-UPDOWN: Interface Serial0/1, changed state to up

Dialer statechange to up Serial0/1Dialer call has been placed Serial0/1
```

4.   According to the **debug** output, what happens on SanJose1 immediately after it attempts to dial 555-6002?

_____

_____

Finally, test the connection by attempting to Telnet from Host B to 192.168.0.1. After the dialup connection is established from SanJose1 to Capetown, the Telnet should be successful. Troubleshoot as necessary.

Chapter 4

ISDN and DDR

Lab 4.9.1: Configuring ISDN BRI

Estimated Time: 50 Minutes

Objective

In this lab, you configure two Cisco routers for dial-on-demand routing (DDR) using ISDN Basic Rate Interface (BRI). You also configure PPP Challenge Handshake Authentication Protocol (CHAP) authentication. Figure 4-1 shows the sample topology you use throughout this lab.

Figure 4-1   Sample Topology for Lab 4.9.1

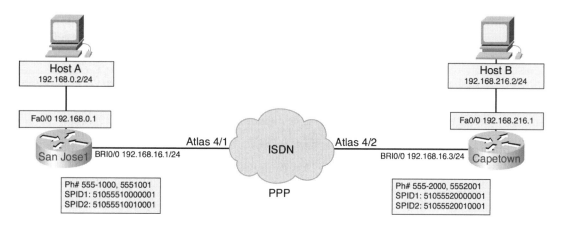

Equipment Requirements

This labs requires an Adtran Atlas 550 or similar device and 2600 or 1700 series routers, as shown in Figure 4-1.

Scenario

The International Travel Agency wants an ISDN DDR connection configured between a remote office in Capetown and its corporate office, known as SanJose1. For security reasons, and to keep ISDN charges to a minimum, the International Travel Agency suggests that only web, e-mail, FTP, Telnet, and Domain Name System (DNS) traffic activate the link from the remote site. Also, it recommends configuring PPP CHAP authentication. Finally, Capetown connects to a stub network. For this reason, the International Travel Agency suggests that you use static and default routes between both sites.

Step 1

Before beginning this lab, reload the routers after erasing their startup configurations. Taking this step prevents problems that residual configurations can cause.

Build and configure the network according to Figure 4-1, but do not configure the BRI interfaces for either router yet. Use the Adtran Atlas 550 or similar device to simulate the ISDN cloud. If you use the Atlas 550, be sure to use straight-through cables. Connect both routers to the respective BRI module ports of the Atlas 550, as labeled in the figure.

Configure the host name and Fast Ethernet 0/0 interfaces on each router.

Configure both workstations with their respective IP addresses and default gateways, such as the router Fa0/0 IP address. Have each host ping its default gateway to verify connectivity.

Step 2

In global configuration mode on SanJose1, use the following to configure the username and password information for the remote router and an enable password for SanJose1:

```
SanJose1(config)#username Capetown password cisco
SanJose1(config)#enable password cisco
SanJose1(config)#line vty 0 4
SanJose1(config-line)#password cisco
SanJose1(config-line)#login
SanJose1(config-line)#exit
```

Note: Normally you use the enable secret password here, but for the purposes of this lab, all you need is an enable password. Later in the lab, you perform a Telnet to SanJose1; therefore, the virtual terminal configuration is necessary.

Configure SanJose1 to use the appropriate ISDN switch type. The Internet service provider (ISP) provides this information, and in this case, it told the International Travel Agency that it is using the National switch type. Enter the following command:

```
SanJose1(config)#isdn switch-type basic-ni
```

Next, set up a dialer list to use with DDR. This dialer list identifies interesting traffic, that is, traffic for which the ISDN link should be established. The International Travel Agency wants to restrict what constitutes "interesting" traffic. However, at this time, use the following command:

```
SanJose1(config)#dialer-list 1 protocol ip permit
```

This permissive command establishes the link for any IP traffic that you need to route out the BRI interface. In Step 6, you reconfigure this dialer list to fulfill the client's requirements completely.

Finally, configure a static route to the Capetown stub network (192.168.216.0/24) as follows:

```
SanJose1(config)#ip route 192.168.216.0 255.255.255.0 192.168.16.3
```

Step 3

Configure the SanJose1 BRI interface with IP address, encapsulation, and authentication settings as follows:

```
SanJose1(config)#interface bri0/0
SanJose1(config-if)#ip address 192.168.16.1 255.255.255.0
SanJose1(config-if)#encapsulation ppp
SanJose1(config-if)#ppp authentication chap
```

For this BRI to establish a connection with the service provider's ISDN switch, configure at least one service profile identifier (SPID). With two B channels, configure two SPIDs. Enter the following commands on SanJose1:

```
SanJose1(config-if)#isdn spid1 51055510000001 5551000
SanJose1(config-if)#isdn spid2 51055510010001 5551001
```

Organizations are typically charged by the minute when making a DDR call. Therefore, it is very important to consider changing the dialer idle-timeout default value of 120 seconds to a lower value. If the connection is idle, the router waits for this configurable period of time before closing the connection. The International Travel Agency wants you to set an aggressive idle timeout to reduce costs. Use the following command to change the timer:

```
SanJose1(config-if)#dialer idle-timeout 60
```

Next, configure the DDR setting on the BRI interface. Use the **dialer-group 1** command as follows, to associate this interface with the already configured **dialer-list 1**:

```
SanJose1(config-if)#dialer-group 1
```

The DDR uses the **dialer map** command whenever the interface encounters interesting traffic. Now, configure the **dialer map** for this interface:

```
SanJose1(config-if)#dialer map ip 192.168.16.3 name Capetown 5552000
```

Notice that this **dialer map** command is similar to the dialer maps that you created in previous labs. However, because you do not use a modem, no modem-script is required.

Finally, activate the BRI 0/0 interface with the **no shutdown** command. After you activate the BRI interface, the router sends the SPIDs to the ISDN switch. Informational messages should appear on the screen stating that the status of the BRI 0/0 is up, but its B channels, BRI 0/0:1, BRI 0/0:2, are down. The following messages state that the terminal endpoint identifiers (TEIs) are up and should be received:

```
01:26:09: %LINK-3-UPDOWN: Interface BRI0/0:1, changed state to down
01:26:09: %LINK-3-UPDOWN: Interface BRI0/0:2, changed state to down
01:26:09: %LINK-3-UPDOWN: Interface BRI0/0, changed state to up
01:26:09: %ISDN-6-LAYER2UP: Layer 2 for Interface BR0/0, TEI 64 changed to up
01:26:09: %ISDN-6-LAYER2UP: Layer 2 for Interface BR0/0, TEI 65 changed to up
```

If the preceding messages do not appear, or error messages appear, troubleshoot as necessary.

Next, use the **show isdn status** command to get more specific information regarding the established connection with the ISDN switch. The following shows a sample output:

```
SanJose1#show isdn status
Global ISDN Switchtype = basic-ni
ISDN BRI0/0 interface
    dsl 0, interface ISDN Switchtype = basic-ni
    Layer 1 Status:
    ACTIVE
    Layer 2 Status:
    TEI = 64, Ces = 1, SAPI = 0, State = MULTIPLE FRAME ESTABLISHED
    TEI = 65, Ces = 2, SAPI = 0, State = MULTIPLE_FRAME_ESTABLISHED
    Spid Status:
    TEI 64, ces = 1, state = 8(established)
        spid1 configured, spid1 sent, spid1 valid
        Endpoint ID Info: epsf = 0, usid = 70, tid = 1
    TEI 65, ces = 2, state = 8(established)
        spid2 configured, spid2 sent, spid2 valid
        Endpoint ID Info: epsf = 0, usid = 70, tid = 2
    Layer 3 Status:
    0 Active Layer 3 Call(s)
    Activated dsl 0 CCBs = 0
    The Free Channel Mask:  0x80000003
    Total Allocated ISDN CCBs = 0
```

If the SPID status is not established or if the SPID configuration on the router is changed, issue the **clear interface** command to force the router to resend the SPID to the switch. Executing this command once should be sufficient. However, when using the Atlas 550 with the Cisco IOS, it might be necessary to repeat the command a second or third time:

```
SanJose1#clear interface bri0/0
```

You can also use the **debug isdn q921** command to troubleshoot Layer 2 issues between the router and the ISDN switch.

After you verify connectivity to the ISDN switch, issue the **show interface bri0/0** command, as follows:

```
SanJose1#show interface bri0/0
BRI0/0 is up, line protocol is up (spoofing)
Hardware is PQUICC BRI with U interface
Internet address is 10.1.1.1/24
MTU 1500 bytes, BW 64 Kbit, DLY 20000 usec,
    reliability 255/255, txload 1/255, rxload 1/255
Encapsulation PPP, loopback not set
<output omitted>
```

The highlighted portion of the output shows that the BRI0/0 interface is up and the line protocol is up or spoofing:

1. You have not yet made an ISDN call, so why did the BRI show "up and up" (spoofing)?

_____

_____

Now, issue the **show ip interface brief** command, as follows:

```
SanJose1#show ip interface brief
Interface          IP-Address     OK?   Method          Status
      Protocol
FastEthernet0/0    192.168.0.1    YES   manual            up           up
Serial0/0          unassigned     YES   unset     down               down
BRI0/0             192.168.16.1         YES   manual              up           up
BRI0/0:1           unassigned     YES   unset     down       down
BRI0/0:2           unassigned     YES   unset     down       down
Serial0/1          unassigned     YES   unset     down       down
```

2. What do BRI0/0:1 and BRI0/0:2 refer to?

_____

_____

3. Why is BRI0/0 up and BRI0/0:1 down?

_____

_____

Issue the **show dialer** command. The following shows a sample output:

```
SanJose1#show dialer
BRI0/0 - dialer type = ISDN

Dial String      Successes   Failures     Last DNIS    Last status
0 incoming call(s) have been screened.
0 incoming call(s) rejected for callback.
```

```
BRI0/0:1 - dialer type = ISDN
Idle timer (60 secs), Fast idle timer (20 secs)
Wait for carrier (30 secs), Re-enable (15 secs)
Dialer state is idle

BRI0/0:2 - dialer type = ISDN
Idle timer (60 secs), Fast idle timer (20 secs)
Wait for carrier (30 secs), Re-enable (15 secs)
Dialer state is idle
```

4.   What is the idle timer set to for both BRI0/0:1 and BRI0/0:2?

_____

_____

Step 4

Now, configure the Capetown router. The steps to accomplish this process are basically the same as Steps 2 through 3. Therefore, complete the following:

```
Capetown(config)#isdn switch-type basic-ni
Capetown(config)#username SanJose1 password cisco
Capetown(config)#enable password cisco
Capetown(config)#line vty 0 4
Capetown(config-line)#password cisco
Capetown(config-line)#login
Capetown(config-line)#exit
Capetown(config)#interface bri0/0
Capetown(config-if)#ip address 192.168.16.3 255.255.255.0
Capetown(config-if)#encapsulation ppp
Capetown(config-if)#ppp authentication chap
Capetown(config-if)#dialer-group 1
Capetown(config-if)#isdn spid1 51055520000001 5552000
Capetown(config-if)#isdn spid2 51055520010001 5552001
Capetown(config-if)#dialer idle-timeout 60
Capetown(config-if)#dialer map ip 192.168.16.1 name SanJose1 5551000
Capetown(config-if)#no shutdown
```

Capetown is a stub network. All traffic destined for other networks other than its own should be forwarded to SanJose1. For this reason, enter a default static route on Capetown pointing to SanJose1 as follows:

```
Capetown(config)#ip route 0.0.0.0 0.0.0.0 192.168.16.1
```

Finally, to test and confirm connectivity between both sites, configure a more permissive dialer list as follows:

```
Capetown(config)#dialer-list 1 protocol ip permit
```

After you confirm connectivity between the two routers, you configure a more restrictive dialer list on Capetown.

Step 5

Test the ISDN connection. Before bringing up the ISDN link, enable debugging on both routers so you can troubleshoot more efficiently if you encounter problems. Issue the following command to view dialer information on both routers:

```
SanJose1#debug dialer
```

You might need to debug the ISDN with the following command:

```
SanJose1#debug isdn events
```

Finally, because you are using PPP with CHAP authentication, debug PPP as follows:

```
SanJose1#debug ppp authentication
SanJose1#debug ppp negotiation
```

Now, ping Host A from Host B. You see a number of debug outputs. They include a dialer debug on Capetown that should report the following:

```
00:56:00: BRI0/0 DDR: Dialing cause ip (s=192.168.216.2, d=192.168.0.2)
00:56:00: BRI0/0 DDR: Attempting to dial 5551000
```

Also, Capetown should report that channel B1 is now up, as the following shows:

```
00:56:01: %LINEPROTO-5-UPDOWN:Line protocol on Interface BRI0/0:1,changed
state to up
00:56:06: %ISDN-6-CONNECT: Interface BRI0/0:1 is now connected to 5551000
SanJose1
```

Troubleshoot this connection as necessary. Use the debug output for clues. You might need to use the **clear interface bri0/0** command several times on both routers to reset the interfaces.

Note: To manually disconnect an ISDN call on BRI0/0, use the following command:

```
SanJose1#isdn disconnect interface bri0/0 [all, b1, b2]
```

Continue testing the ISDN connection; ping Host A from Host B and Host B from Host A.

You can also issue the **show isdn history** command to view all active and prior ISDN connections. The **show isdn active** command outputs information about the current active connection. The following are sample outputs of both commands:

```
SanJose1#show isdn history
```

```
--------------------------------------------------------------------------
                            ISDN CALL HISTORY
--------------------------------------------------------------------------
History table has a maximum of 100 entries.
History table data is retained for a maximum of 15 Minutes.
--------------------------------------------------------------------------
```

Call Type	Calling Number	Called Number	Remote Name	Seconds Used	Seconds Left	Seconds Idle	Charges Units/Currency
Out	---N/A---	5551000	Capetown	60			
Out	---N/A---	5551000	Capetown	40	19	40	

```
--------------------------------------------------------------------------
```

```
Capetown#show isdn active
```

```
--------------------------------------------------------------------------
                            ISDN ACTIVE CALLS
--------------------------------------------------------------------------
History table has a maximum of 100 entries.
History table data is retained for a maximum of 15 Minutes.
--------------------------------------------------------------------------
```

Call Type	Calling Number	Called Number	Remote Name	Seconds Used	Seconds Left	Seconds Idle	Charges Units/Currency
Out		5551000	SanJose1	18	44	15	0

```
--------------------------------------------------------------------------
```

Step 6

Now that there is a working ISDN connection, configure a more restrictive dialer list on the Capetown remote router to keep ISDN charges to a minimum.

Create an access list to specifically permit web, DNS, FTP, Telnet, and mail traffic. Reconfigure dialer list 1 on Capetown, the remote router. The central site router, SanJose1, continues to be allowed to establish DDR connections for any IP traffic.

Use the following to create an access list on Capetown that permits the mission-critical services:

```
Capetown(config)#access-list 101 permit tcp any any eq www
Capetown(config)#access-list 101 permit udp any any eq domain
Capetown(config)#access-list 101 permit tcp any any eq ftp
Capetown(config)#access-list 101 permit tcp any any eq telnet
Capetown(config)#access-list 101 permit tcp any any eq pop3
Capetown(config)#access-list 101 permit tcp any any eq smtp
```

Note: This code uses transport layer keywords instead of port numbers. Layer 4 keyword services are simpler to interpret when you configure extended access lists. Use the **?** option after the **eq** parameter to receive a list of keywords and their associated port numbers.

Now enter a new **dialer-list** command that references this access list. The following shows a new **dialer-list** command automatically replacing the old one:

```
Capetown(config)#dialer-list 1 protocol ip list 101
```

After you configure the new dialer list, ping Host A from Host B.

1.   The ping should fail; why?

_____

_____

From Host B, initiate a Telnet session to SanJose1.

2.   The Telnet request should bring up the ISDN connection; why?

_____

_____

With the connection still up, ping Host A from Host B once again.

3.   Instead of failing as before, this ping should work. Why?

_____

_____

A ping to Host B from Host A should also be possible.

While connected, issue the **show dialer** command on both SanJose1 and Capetown.

4.   According to the output of this command, what was the time until disconnect for SanJose1?

_____

Lab 4.9.2: Configuring Snapshot Routing

Estimated Time: 45 Minutes

Objective

In this lab, you configure two Cisco routers for DDR and snapshot routing using ISDN BRI.
Figure 4-2 shows the sample topology you use. (This sample topology is the same as that shown
in Figure 4-1.)

Figure 4-2   Sample Topology for Lab 4.9.2

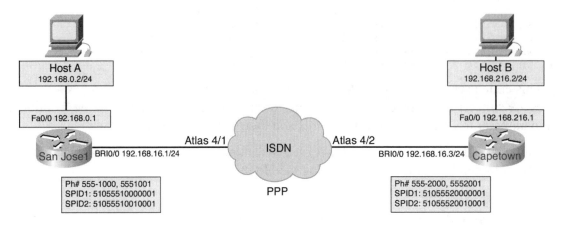

Equipment Requirements

This lab requires an Adtran Atlas 550 or similar device and 2600 or 1700 series routers, as
shown in Figure 4-2.

Scenario

The International Travel Agency wants an ISDN DDR connection configured between its
Capetown regional headquarters and the corporate network SanJose1 core router. Instead of
configuring static routes, configure snapshot routing so that routing updates are exchanged
between the routers without keeping the link up continuously. The company has also asked you
to configure PPP encapsulation and CHAP authentication over this link.

Step 1

Before beginning this lab, reload the routers after erasing their startup configurations. Taking this
step prevents problems that residual configurations can cause. Build and configure the network
according to Figure 4-2, but do not configure the BRI interfaces on either router yet. Use the
Adtran Atlas 550 or similar device to simulate the ISDN cloud. If you use the Atlas 550, be sure
to use straight-through cables and connect both routers to the respective BRI module ports of the
Atlas 550, as labeled in the figure. Be sure to configure both workstations with the correct IP
address and default gateway. Configure the Fa0/0 interfaces of the routers to match the diagram.

Step 2

Configure SanJose1 and Capetown for ISDN. Refer to the following commands to guide the
configuration:

```
SanJose1(config)#username Capetown password cisco
SanJose1(config)#enable password cisco
```

```
SanJose1(config)#line vty 0 4
SanJose1(config-line)#password cisco
SanJose1(config-line)#login
SanJose1(config-line)#exit
SanJose1(config)#isdn switch-type basic-ni
SanJose1(config)#dialer-list 1 protocol ip permit
SanJose1(config)#interface bri0/0
SanJose1(config-if)#ip address 192.168.16.1 255.255.255.0
SanJose1(config-if)#encapsulation ppp
SanJose1(config-if)#ppp authentication chap
SanJose1(config-if)#isdn spid1 51055510000001 5551000
SanJose1(config-if)#isdn spid2 51055510010001 5551001
SanJose1(config-if)#dialer-group 1
SanJose1(config-if)#dialer map ip 192.168.16.3 name Capetown 5552000
SanJose1(config-if)#no shutdown

Capetown(config)#username SanJose1 password cisco
Capetown(config)#enable password cisco
Capetown(config)#line vty 0 4
Capetown(config-line)#password cisco
Capetown(config-line)#login
Capetown(config-line)#exit
Capetown(config)#isdn switch-type basic-ni
Capetown(config)#dialer-list 1 protocol ip permit
Capetown(config)#interface bri0/0
Capetown(config-if)#ip address 192.168.16.3 255.255.255.0
Capetown(config-if)#encapsulation ppp
Capetown(config-if)#ppp authentication chap
Capetown(config-if)#isdn spid1 51055520000001 5552000
Capetown(config-if)#isdn spid2 51055520010001 5552001
Capetown(config-if)#dialer-group 1
Capetown(config-if)#dialer map ip 192.168.16.1 name SanJose1 5551000
Capetown(config-if)#no shutdown
```

1.   What does the keyword **broadcast** do when you use it with the **dialer map** command?

_____

_____

Use the **show isdn status** command to verify that the routers have established communication with the ISDN switch.

If either of the routers has not established communication with the ISDN switch, check the running configuration file to verify that you entered the configurations correctly. You can also use the **clear interface bri0/0** command multiple times if necessary to enable a valid and established SPID status.

Step 3

After you properly configure both routers for ISDN, issue the **debug dialer** command on both SanJose1 and Capetown. Then, verify that DDR works by pinging SanJose1, 192.168.16.1, from Capetown. You can also use the **show isdn active** command to verify an active connection. Troubleshoot as necessary.

Leave **debug dialer** enabled. You use the output of this command in Step 4.

Step 4

This lab does not use static routes. The International Travel Agency has asked that you configure dynamic routing. This setup will allow routing table updates to occur automatically as it adds new networks.

1.   How often does Interior Gateway Routing Protocol (IGRP) send updates by default?

_____

_____

2.   Are IGRP updates unicast, multicast, or broadcast?

_____

_____

3.   What is the default setting of **dialer idle-timeout**?

_____

_____

Starting with SanJose1, configure IGRP for AS 100 on both SanJose1 and Capetown. The following are commands for SanJose1:

```
SanJose1(config)#router igrp 100
SanJose1(config-router)#network 192.168.0.0
SanJose1(config-router)#network 192.168.16.0
```

The following are commands for Capetown:

```
Capetown(config)#router igrp 100
Capetown(config-router)#network 192.168.16.0
Capetown(config-router)#network 192.168.216.0
```

Issue the **show ip route** command on Capetown to verify its routing table as follows:

```
Capetown#show ip route
Codes: C - connected, S - static, I - IGRP, R - RIP, M - mobile, B - BGP
       D - EIGRP, EX - EIGRP external, O - OSPF, IA - OSPF inter area
       N1 - OSPF NSSA external type 1, N2 - OSPF NSSA external type 2
       E1 - OSPF external type 1, E2 - OSPF external type 2, E - EGP
       i - IS-IS, L1 - IS-IS level-1,L2 - IS-IS level-2, ia - IS-IS inter area
       * - candidate default, U - per-user static route, o - ODR
       P - periodic downloaded static route
Gateway of last resort is not set
C    192.168.216.0/24 is directly connected, FastEthernet0/0
     192.168.16.0/24 is variably subnetted, 2 subnets, 2 masks
C       192.168.16.0/24 is directly connected, BRI0/0
C       192.168.16.1/32 is directly connected, BRI0/0
```

Notice that IGRP has not detected the Ethernet network of SanJose1. The reason is the dialer map statements that you entered on each router. IGRP builds its routing table based on broadcasts received by a peer. By default, the dialer map statements you entered do not allow broadcast traffic to leave the interface.

For this reason, the **dialer map** command must include the optional **broadcast** keyword. On the BRI 0/0 interface of each router, enter the respective **dialer map** statements as follows:

```
SanJose1(config-if)#dialer map ip 192.168.16.3 name Capetown broadcast 5552000
Capetown(config-if)#dialer map ip 192.168.16.1 name SanJose1 broadcast 5551000
```

After you configure the dialer maps, you should see DDR activity, as generated by the **debug dialer** command. The output from this command should be similar to the following:

```
BRI0/0 DDR: Dialing cause ip (s=192.168.16.3, d=255.255.255.255)
BRI0/0 DDR: Attempting to dial 5551000
```

4. According to the debug output, what is the destination of the packet that caused the attempt to dial?

_____

_____

5. What process on the router is causing this broadcast packet to be generated?

_____

_____

6. Under the current configuration, this DDR link should never go down. Why?

_____

_____

With IGRP, the router broadcasts routing updates out every interface configured with IGRP. Therefore, IGRP broadcast routing updates consistently keep the DDR link active.

Because an IGRP routing process is initiating a DDR call, you can assume that IGRP routing updates are being exchanged between SanJose1 and Capetown. To verify this assumption, issue the **show ip route** command again as follows:

```
Capetown#show ip route
Codes: C - connected, S - static, I - IGRP, R - RIP, M - mobile, B - BGP
       D - EIGRP, EX - EIGRP external, O - OSPF, IA - OSPF inter area
       N1 - OSPF NSSA external type 1, N2 - OSPF NSSA external type 2
       E1 - OSPF external type 1, E2 - OSPF external type 2, E - EGP
       i - IS-IS, L1 - IS-IS level-1, L2 - IS-IS level-2, ia - IS-IS inter
area
       * - candidate default, U - per-user static route, o - ODR
       P - periodic downloaded static route
Gateway of last resort is not set
C    192.168.216.0/24 is directly connected, FastEthernet0/0
I    192.168.0.0/24 [100/158260] via 192.168.16.1, 00:00:10, BRI0/0
     192.168.16.0/24 is variably subnetted, 2 subnets, 2 masks
C       192.168.16.0/24 is directly connected, BRI0/0
C       192.168.16.1/32 is directly connected, BRI0/0
```

Notice that the routers have converged and that Capetown now knows about the SanJose1 Ethernet network.

Step 5

Configure snapshot routing. As the core router, SanJose1 acts as the server and Capetown is the client. Issue the following commands on SanJose1:

```
SanJose1(config)#interface bri0/0
SanJose1(config-if)#snapshot server 5
```

The **snapshot server 5** command tells the server that the active period is 5 minutes long.

1.   What is the maximum interval that you can assign using the **snapshot server** command?

Note: You can use the help feature to find this answer.

Now, use the following to configure Capetown as a snapshot routing client:

```
Capetown(config)#interface bri0/0
Capetown(config-if)#dialer map snapshot 1 name SanJose1 broadcast 5551000
Capetown(config-if)#snapshot client 5 10 suppress-statechange-update dialer
```

The **dialer map snapshot** command establishes a map that Capetown uses to connect for exchanging routing updates with SanJose1. The **snapshot client** command configures the length of the active and quiet periods. In the previous command, you set the active period to 5 minutes. This value must match the value set in the configuration for the snapshot server. You set the length of the quiet period to 10 minutes.

By default, snapshot routing takes advantage of each new connection that enters into an active window and starts the active interval every time. This arrangement could be problem in situations where the WAN link is accessed often and where some applications require only a short connection time of less than a minute.

The **suppress-statechange-update** keyword prevents the routers from exchanging updates during connections that are established to transfer user data. This setup allows snapshot routing to initiate the DDR link, thereby starting an active period at the expiration of the quiet period.

The **dialer** keyword allows the client router to dial up the server router in the absence of regular traffic. Also, it is required when you use the **suppress-statechange-update** keyword.

Observe the result of this configuration. If the routers are still connected, use the **show dialer** command to determine how long the routers wait until they disconnect an idle link.

Let the link remain idle for 120 seconds. After that time, the routers should disconnect.

Check the routing tables of SanJose1 and Capetown. Verify that routing is working within this network by pinging SanJose1, 192.168.16.1, from Capetown.

Issue the **show snapshot** command on both routers. Notice that the output of SanJose1 differs significantly from the output of Capetown, as the following shows:

```
SanJose1#show snapshot
BRI0/0 is up, line protocol is up, Snapshot server line state down
  Length of active period:        5 minutes
    For ip address: 192.168.16.3
      Current state: active, remaining time: 5 minutes

Capetown#show snapshot
BRI0/0 is up, line protocol is up, Snapshot client
  Options: dialer support, stay asleep on carrier up
  Length of active period:        5 minutes
  Length of quiet period:         10 minutes
  Length of retry period:         8 minutes
   For dialer address 1
     Current state: active, remaining/exchange time: 5/0 minutes
     Connected dialer interface:
       BRI0/0:1
```

2.   According to the output of this command, what is the retry period set to?

_____

_____

After allowing the connection to time out, wait 5 minutes with **debug dialer** running on each router. The following are sample outputs for SanJose1 and Capetown when snapshot routing is activated:

```
SanJose1#debug dialer
01:21:49: %LINK-3-UPDOWN: Interface BRI0/0:1, changed state to up
01:21:49: %ISDN-6-CONNECT: Interface BRI0/0:1 is now connected to unknown
01:21:49: isdn_call_connect: Calling line action of BRI0/0:1
01:21:49: BRI0/0:1 DDR: Authenticated host Capetown with no matching dialer
  map
01:21:49: BR0/0:1 DDR: Dialer protocol up
01:21:49: BRI0/0:1 DDR: dialer protocol up
01:21:4w9: BRI0/0: dialer_ckt_swt_client_connect: incoming circuit switched
  call
01:21:50: %LINEPROTO-5-UPDOWN: Line protocol on Interface BRI0/0:1, changed
  state to up
01:21:55: %ISDN-6-CONNECT: Interface BRI0/0:1 is now connected to  Capetown

Capetown#debug dialer
00:29:27282767: isdn_call_connect: Calling line action of BRI0/0:1
00:29:00: BRI0/0:1 DDR: Authenticated host SanJose1 with no matching dialer
  map
00:29:00: BR0/0:1 DDR: Dialer protocol up
00:29:00: BRI0/0:1 DDR: dialer protocol up
00:29:00: BRI0/0: dialer_ckt_swt_client_connect: incoming circuit switched
  call
00:29:01: %LINEPROTO-5-UPDOWN: Line protocol on Interface BRI0/0:1, changed
  state to up
00:29:06: %ISDN-6-CONNECT: Interface BRI0/0:1 is now connected to 5551000
  SanJose1
```

3.   Which router dials the other to receive snapshot routing information?

_____

_____

Lab 4.9.3: Using PPP Multilink for ISDN B Channel Aggregation

Estimated Time: 30 Minutes

Objective

In this lab, you configure two Cisco routers for DDR using Multilink PPP (MLP) to use both B channels as a 128 kbps bundle. Figure 4-3 shows the sample topology for this lab.

Figure 4-3   Sample Topology for Lab 4.9.3

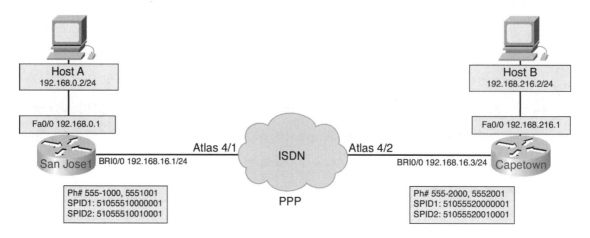

Equipment Requirements

This lab requires an Adtran Atlas 550 or similar device and 2600 or 1700 series routers, as shown in Figure 4-3.

Scenario

The International Travel Agency wants you to configure an ISDN DDR connection between a remote office in Capetown and its corporate office, known as SanJose1. To maximize bandwidth, configure MLP to use both B channels for the data link.

Step 1

Before beginning this lab, reload the routers after erasing their startup configurations. Taking this step prevents problems that residual configurations might cause.

Build and configure the network according to Figure 4-3, but do not configure the BRI interfaces on either router yet. Use the Adtran Atlas 550 or similar device to simulate the ISDN cloud. If you use the Atlas 550, be sure to use straight-through cables. Connect both routers to the respective BRI module ports of the Atlas 550, as labeled in the figure. Be sure to configure both workstations with the correct IP address and default gateway.

Step 2

Configure SanJose1 and Capetown for ISDN. Refer to the following commands to guide the configuration:

```
SanJose1(config)#username Capetown password cisco
SanJose1(config)#isdn switch-type basic-ni
SanJose1(config)#interface bri0/0
```

```
SanJose1(config-if)#ip address 192.168.16.1 255.255.255.0
SanJose1(config-if)#encapsulation ppp
SanJose1(config-if)#ppp authentication chap
SanJose1(config-if)#isdn spid1 51055510000001 5551000
SanJose1(config-if)#isdn spid2 51055510010001 5551001
SanJose1(config-if)#dialer idle-timeout 60
SanJose1(config-if)#dialer-group 1
SanJose1(config-if)#dialer map ip 192.168.16.3 name Capetown 5552000
SanJose1(config-if)#no shutdown
SanJose1(config)#dialer-list 1 protocol ip permit
SanJose1(config)#ip route 192.168.216.0 255.255.255.0 192.168.16.3

Capetown(config)#enable password cisco
Capetown(config)#line vty 0 4
Capetown(config-line)#password cisco
Capetown(config-line)#exit
Capetown(config)#username SanJose1 password cisco
Capetown(config)#isdn switch-type basic-ni
Capetown(config)#interface bri0/0
Capetown(config-if)#ip address 192.168.16.3 255.255.255.0
Capetown(config-if)#encapsulation ppp
Capetown(config-if)#ppp authentication chap
Capetown(config-if)#isdn spid1 51055520000001 5552000
Capetown(config-if)#isdn spid2 51055520010001 5552001
Capetown(config-if)#dialer idle-timeout 60
Capetown(config-if)#dialer-group 1
Capetown(config-if)#dialer map ip 192.168.16.1 name SanJose1 5551000
Capetown(config-if)#no shutdown
Capetown(config)#dialer-list 1 protocol ip permit
Capetown(config)#ip route 0.0.0.0 0.0.0.0 192.168.16.1
```

Use the **show isdn status** command to verify that the routers have established communication with the ISDN switch. If the routers have not established communication with the ISDN switch, use the **clear interface bri0/0** command multiple times, if necessary, to enable a valid and established SPID status. You can also use the **show running-config** command on each router to verify that you entered the configurations correctly.

Verify that the routers have established communication with the ISDN switch with the **show isdn status** command. Use the **clear interface bri0/0** command multiple times if necessary to enable a valid and established SPID status.

Issue the **debug dialer** command on both SanJose1 and Capetown. Then, test the DDR configuration by pinging Host A from Host B. Troubleshoot as necessary.

Step 3

Configure each router for multilink PPP. On both SanJose1 and Capetown, issue the following commands for PPP multilink:

```
SanJose1(config)#interface bri0/0
SanJose1(config-if)#ppp multilink
SanJose1(config-if)#dialer load-threshold 1 either
SanJose1(config-if)#dialer map ip 192.168.16.3 name Capetown 5552001
SanJose1(config-if)#dialer redial interval 5 attempts 3

Capetown(config)#interface bri0/0
Capetown(config-if)#ppp multilink
Capetown(config-if)#dialer load-threshold 1 either
Capetown(config-if)#dialer map ip 192.168.16.1 name SanJose1 5551001
Capetown(config-if)#dialer redial interval 5 attempts 3
```

You use the **ppp multilink** command on ISDN interfaces to bundle both 64 kbps B channels. When bundled, they function together as a 128 kbps pipe.

The **dialer load-threshold** command specifies how much traffic on the first B channel forces the second channel to be brought up. This command takes a numerical argument from 1 to 255. The number 1 is the minimum load and enables the second channel automatically. The number 255 is a full load. Therefore, the value 128 is approximately a 50% load.

If the threshold is set to 255, the second B channel is not brought up until the first channel is completely loaded. By default, only outbound traffic is monitored. To monitor incoming and outgoing traffic, you use the keyword **either**. The option of specifying **inbound** or **outbound** instead is also available.

Enter a second dialer map statement to map the Layer 3 IP address to another Layer 2 destination SPID. Essentially, it configures the second B channel.

The **dialer redial** command was introduced in Cisco IOS Software Release 12.1(2). Therefore, this command is not available, and not required, if you use an older Cisco IOS version. The command sets the redial interval between dial attempts to 5 seconds, for a maximum of three attempts. This interval allows for the old call to be torn down completely before the redial is attempted.

Step 4

Ping Host A from Host B. This ping should bring up the DDR connection. Troubleshoot as necessary.

After the connection is up, verify that both channels are enabled. Use the **show ip interface brief** command on both routers. Notice that both B channels are up. If only channel 1 is up, clear the interface and send more pings to Host A from Host B. The following are sample outputs:

```
SanJose1#show ip interface brief
Interface               IP-Address      OK? Method Status
Protocol
FastEthernet0/0         192.168.0.1     YES NVRAM  up                        up
Serial0/0               unassigned      YES NVRAM  administratively down down
BRI0/0                  192.168.16.1    YES NVRAM  up                        up
BRI0/0:1                unassigned      YES unset  up                        up
BRI0/0:2                unassigned      YES unset  up                        up
Serial0/1               unassigned      YES NVRAM  administratively down down
Virtual-Access1         unassigned      YES TFTP   up                        up

Capetown#show ip interface brief
Interface               IP-Address      OK? Method Status
Protocol
FastEthernet0/0         192.168.216.1   YES NVRAM  up                        up
Serial0/0               unassigned      YES NVRAM  administratively down down
BRI0/0                  192.168.16.3    YES NVRAM  up                        up
BRI0/0:1                unassigned      YES unset  up                        up
BRI0/0:2                unassigned      YES unset  up                        up
Serial0/1               unassigned      YES NVRAM  administratively down down
Virtual-Access1         unassigned      YES TFTP   up                        up
```

Notice that both B channels show "up and up."

1. A new interface appeared in the output from the **show ip interface brief** command. What is it called?

_____

With the ISDN connection still active, issue the **show dialer** command on both routers. The following are sample outputs:

```
SanJose1#show dialer
BRI0/0 - dialer type = ISDN
Dial String      Successes    Failures    Last DNIS    Last status
0 incoming call(s) have been screened.
0 incoming call(s) rejected for callback.

BRI0/0:1 - dialer type = ISDN
Idle timer (60 secs), Fast idle timer (20 secs)
Wait for carrier (30 secs), Re-enable (15 secs)
Dialer state is multilink member (Capetown)

BRI0/0:2 - dialer type = ISDN
Idle timer (60 secs), Fast idle timer (20 secs)
Wait for carrier (30 secs), Re-enable (15 secs)
Dialer state is multilink member
Connected to <unknown phone number> (Capetown)

Capetown#show dialer
BRI0/0 - dialer type = ISDN
Dial String      Successes    Failures    Last DNIS    Last status
5551001               0           0        never             -
5551000              21           0        00:00:31     successful
0 incoming call(s) have been screened.
0 incoming call(s) rejected for callback.

BRI0/0:1 - dialer type = ISDN
Idle timer (60 secs), Fast idle timer (20 secs)
Wait for carrier (30 secs), Re-enable (15 secs)
Dialer state is multilink member
Dial reason: ip (s=192.168.216.2, d=192.168.0.2)
Connected to 5551000 (SanJose1)

BRI0/0:2 - dialer type = ISDN
Idle timer (60 secs), Fast idle timer (20 secs)
Wait for carrier (30 secs), Re-enable (15 secs)
Dialer state is multilink member
Dial reason: Multilink bundle overloaded
Connected to 5551000 (SanJose1)
```

2. Which part of the **show dialer** command output indicated that PPP multilink is functioning?

_____

_____

3. What was the dial reason for the first B channel? What was the dial reason for the second B channel?

_____

_____

Issue the **show ppp multilink** command on SanJose1 and on Capetown. The following are sample outputs:

```
SanJose1#show ppp multilink
Virtual-Access1, bundle name is Capetown
  Dialer interface is BRI0/0
  0 lost fragments, 0 reordered, 0 unassigned, sequence 0x3/0x0 rcvd/sent
  0 discarded, 0 lost received, 1/255 load
  Member links: 2 (max not set, min not set)
    BRI0/0:1
    BRI0/0:2

Capetown#show ppp multilink
Virtual-Access1, bundle name is SanJose1
  Dialer interface is BRI0/0
  0 lost fragments, 0 reordered, 0 unassigned, sequence 0x0/0x6 rcvd/sent
  0 discarded, 0 lost received, 1/255 load
  Member links: 2 (max not set, min not set)
    BRI0/0:1
    BRI0/0:2
```

4.   According to the output of this command, how many channels are participating in the bundle?

_____

_____

Lab 4.9.4: Configuring ISDN PRI

Estimated Time: 30 Minutes

Objective

In this lab, you configure ISDN BRI on the remote site routers and ISDN Primary Rate Interface (PRI) on the central site router. Figure 4-4 shows the sample topology.

Figure 4-4   Sample Topology for Lab 4.9.4

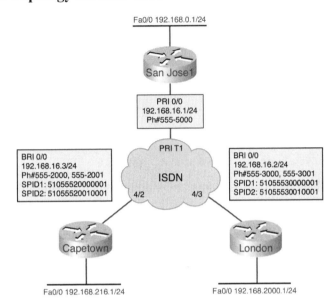

Equipment Requirements

This lab requires an Adtran Atlas 550 or similar device and 2600 or 1700 series routers, as shown in Figure 4-4.

Scenario

The International Travel Agency wants you to configure a connection between remote offices in Capetown and London and its corporate network router in SanJose1. The corporate office has just had an ISDN PRI provisioned so that SanJose1 can handle 23 ISDN BRI or V.90 asynchronous dialup calls simultaneously. You need to configure the BRIs on the remote routers and the T1 controller and PRI D channel on SanJose1. When the configuration is complete, each router should be able to dial the other two routers. SanJose1 should be able to receive calls from both London and Capetown.

Step 1

Before beginning this lab, you should reload the routers after erasing their startup configurations. Taking this step prevents problems that residual configurations can cause. This lab assumes that SanJose1 has a T1 controller module installed. Build and configure the network according to Figure 4-4, but do not configure the PRI and BRI interfaces on either router yet. Use the Adtran Atlas 550 or similar device to simulate the ISDN cloud. If you use the Atlas 550, be sure to use straight-through cables. Connect both routers to the BRI module ports of the Atlas 550, as labeled in the figure. Connect the T1 controller on SanJose1 to the T1 PRI port on the Atlas 550.

This connection might require a DB-15-to-RJ-45 adapter on the T1 controller module and the appropriate cable supplied with the Atlas 550.

Step 2

Configure the ISDN PRI connection. Specify the ISDN PRI switch type, which is determined by the carrier. The ISDN service provider connecting SanJose1 is using a Northern Telecom DMS100. The switch is running the National ISDN, Version 1, software that is identified by the keyword **primary-ni**. Enter the following command:

```
SanJose1(config)#isdn switch-type primary-ni
```

Next, configure the local username and password database so that SanJose1 can authenticate the remote routers with CHAP as follows:

```
SanJose1(config)#username Capetown password cisco
SanJose1(config)#username London password cisco
```

Specify what types of traffic will generate a call to the remote router. Configure a dialer list to specify any IP traffic as interesting with the following command:

```
SanJose1(config)#dialer-list 1 protocol ip permit
```

The SanJose1 router must have a route to both the Capetown and London Ethernet networks. Using the appropriate commands, configure a static route to the LAN for each of these routers.

1.   What are the commands to do this step?

Step 3

In this step, configure the T1 controller. You must configure the controller according to the provider's framing and line coding. In this case, use extended super frame and the binary 8-zero substitution linecode. Also, set the T1 controller to use all timeslots.

Note: Remember that a T1 has 24 64 kbps channels. To configure the PRI controller, issue the following commands:

```
SanJose1(config)#controller t1 1/0
SanJose1(config-controller)#framing esf
SanJose1(config-controller)#linecode b8zs
SanJose1(config-controller)#pri-group timeslots 1-24
```

The final part of the configuration is to configure the PRI D channel. This channel is responsible for call setup and signaling. The D channel uses channel 23, which is the 24th channel because they are numbered beginning with 0. Issue the following commands:

```
SanJose1(config)#interface serial 1/0:23
SanJose1(config-if)#ip address 192.168.16.1 255.255.255.0
SanJose1(config-if)#dialer-group 1
SanJose1(config-if) #dialer load-threshold 1 outbound
SanJose1(config-if)#dialer idle-timeout 60
SanJose1(config-if)#encapsulation ppp
SanJose1(config-if)#ppp multilink
SanJose1(config-if)#ppp authentication chap
```

Configure dialer map statements as follows so that the router knows which numbers to dial to reach specific next-hop IP addresses:

```
SanJose1(config-if)#dialer map ip 192.168.16.3 name Capetown 5552000
SanJose1(config-if)#dialer map ip 192.168.16.3 name Capetown 5552001
SanJose1(config-if)#dialer map ip 192.168.16.2 name London 5553000
SanJose1(config-if)#dialer map ip 192.168.16.2 name London 5553001
```

Finally, use the **show isdn status** command as follows to verify that you have successfully established communication between the router and the ISDN switch:

```
SanJose1#show isdn status
Global ISDN Switchtype = primary-ni
ISDN Serial1/0:23 interface
dsl 0, interface ISDN Switchtype = primary-ni
Layer 1 Status:
ACTIVE
Layer 2 Status:
TEI = 0, Ces = 1, SAPI = 0, State = MULTIPLE_FRAME_ESTABLISHED
Layer 3 Status:
0 Active Layer 3 Call(s)
Activated dsl 0 CCBs = 0
The Free Channel Mask: 0x801FFFFF
Total Allocated ISDN CCBs = 2
```

1.   How is the **show isdn status** output for Layer 2 of a PRI different from a BRI?

Step 4

Configure both of the remote routers to use the appropriate ISDN switch type, National ISDN-1. Because you use PPP encapsulation and CHAP on the B channels, enter username and password information on both routers. The following configuration is for London:

```
London(config)#enable password cisco
London(config)#line vty 0 4
London(config-line)#password cisco
London(config-line)#exit
London(config)#isdn switch-type basic-ni
London(config)#interface bri0/0
London(config)#ip address 192.168.16.2 255.255.255.0
London(config-if)#encapsulation ppp
London(config-if)#ppp authentication chap
London(config-if)#isdn spid1 51055530000001 5553000
London(config-if)#isdn spid2 51055530010001 5553001
London(config-if)#dialer-group 1
London(config-if)#dialer idle-timeout 60
London(config-if)#no shutdown
```

Note: When configuring Capetown, be sure to substitute the appropriate information.

1.   PPP is the line encapsulation on the B channels. What is the encapsulation protocol on the D channel?

Configure dialer-list 1 as follows to identify all IP traffic as interesting on both routers:

```
London(config)#dialer-list 1 protocol ip permit
```

Configure both spoke routers with the username and password of SanJose1 so that they each authenticate SanJose1 using CHAP. You must also configure a static route to the central office LAN on both routers. The following are sample commands for Capetown:

```
Capetown(config)#username SanJose1 password cisco
Capetown(config)#username London password cisco
Capetown(config)#ip route 192.168.0.0 255.255.255.0 192.168.16.1
Capetown(config)#ip route 192.168.200.0 255.255.255.0 192.168.16.2
```

Finally, configure the BRI interfaces for the remote routers with the appropriate dialer map commands. The following are the commands required for Capetown:

```
Capetown(config)#interface bri 0/0
Capetown(config-if)#dialer map ip 192.168.16.1 name SanJose1 5555000
Capetown(config-if)#dialer map ip 192.168.16.2 name London 5553000
Capetown(config-if)#dialer map ip 192.168.16.2 name London 5553001
```

Step 5

Verify the configuration of the Fast Ethernet interface on SanJose1. Ping from both Capetown and London to 192.168.0.1. The pings should be successful. Troubleshoot as necessary.

After the pings, both Capetown and London connect to SanJose1 simultaneously. With multilink configured, Capetown and London should be using both of their B channels.

If either link is disconnected, ping the Fast Ethernet interface on SanJose1 again. After both the Capetown and London links are up, issue the **show ip interface brief** command as follows on SanJose1:

```
SanJose1#show ip interface brief
Interface IP-Address OK? Method Status Protocol
FastEthernet0/0 192.168.0.1 YES NVRAM up up
Serial0/0 unassigned YES NVRAM administratively down down
Serial0/1 unassigned YES NVRAM administratively down down
Serial1/0:0 unassigned YES unset down down
Serial1/0:1 unassigned YES unset down down
Serial1/0:2 unassigned YES unset down down
Serial1/0:3 unassigned YES unset down down
Serial1/0:4 unassigned YES unset down down
Serial1/0:5 unassigned YES unset down down
Serial1/0:6 unassigned YES unset down down
Serial1/0:7 unassigned YES unset down down
Serial1/0:8 unassigned YES unset down down
Serial1/0:9 unassigned YES unset down down
Serial1/0:10 unassigned YES unset down down
Serial1/0:11 unassigned YES unset down down
Serial1/0:12 unassigned YES unset down down
Serial1/0:13 unassigned YES unset down down
Serial1/0:14 unassigned YES unset down down
Serial1/0:15 unassigned YES unset down down
Serial1/0:16 unassigned YES unset down down
Serial1/0:17 unassigned YES unset down down
Serial1/0:18 unassigned YES unset down down
Serial1/0:19 unassigned YES unset up up
Serial1/0:20 unassigned YES unset up up
Serial1/0:21 unassigned YES unset up up
Serial1/0:22 unassigned YES unset up up
Serial1/0:23 192.168.16.1 YES NVRAM up up
Virtual-Access1 unassigned YES TFTP up up
```

1.   According to the output of this command, which channels of the PRI are connected?

_____

_____

2.   Why does Serial1/0:23 have an IP address and not Serial1/0:22 or Serial1/0:20?

_____

With both connections active, issue the **show dialer** command on SanJose1.

3.   What is the dialer reason for Serial1/0:19?

_____

_____

4.   What is the dialer reason for Serial1/0:20?

_____

_____

5.   What is the dialer reason for Serial1/0:21?

_____

_____

6.   What is the dialer reason for Serial1/0:22?

_____

_____

Chapter 5

Dialer Profiles

Lab 5.3.1: Configuring ISDN Using Dialer Profiles

Estimated Time: 45 Minutes

Objective

In this lab, you configure two Cisco routers for ISDN Basic Rate Interface (BRI) using dialer profiles. Figure 5-1 shows the sample topology.

Figure 5-1   Sample Topology for Lab 5.3.1

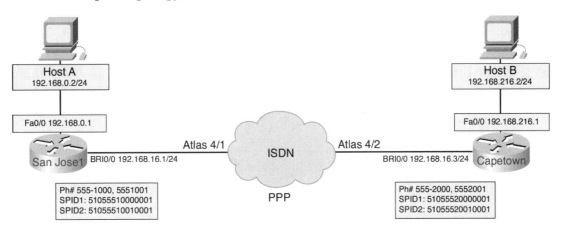

Equipment Requirements

This labs requires an Adtran Atlas 550 or similar device and 2600 or 1700 series routers, as shown in Figure 5-1.

Scenario

The International Travel Agency wants you to configure an ISDN dial-on-demand routing (DDR) connection between a remote office in Capetown and its corporate network core router in SanJose1. It has asked you to configure PPP encapsulation and Challenge Handshake Authentication Protocol (CHAP) authentication over this link. Because the company plans to increase the number of ISDN connections at the central and remote sites, use dialer profiles to simplify future configurations.

Step 1

Before beginning this lab, you should reload the router after erasing its startup configuration. Taking this step prevents problems that residual configurations might cause. Build and configure the network according to Figure 5-1, but do not configure the BRI interfaces for either router yet. Use the Adtran Atlas 550 or a similar device to simulate the ISDN cloud. If you use the Atlas 550, be sure to use straight-through cables. Connect both routers to the BRI module ports of the Atlas 550, as labeled in Figure 5-1. Be sure to configure both workstations with the correct IP address and default gateway. Configure the Fa0/0 interfaces of the routers to match the diagram.

Step 2

Configure both routers to use the appropriate ISDN switch type, National ISDN-1. Because you will use PPP encapsulation and CHAP on the B channels, enter the case-sensitive username and password information on both routers. The following are examples for SanJose1:

```
SanJose1(config)#isdn switch-type basic-ni
SanJose1(config)#username Capetown password cisco
SanJose1(config)#enable password cisco
SanJose1(config)#line vty 0 4
SanJose1(config)#password cisco
SanJose1(config)#login
SanJose1(config)#exit
```

1.   PPP is the line encapsulation on the B channels. What is the encapsulation protocol on the D channel?

_____

_____

Configure **dialer-list 1** to identify all IP traffic as interesting on both routers, as shown in the following:

```
SanJose1(config)#dialer-list 1 protocol ip permit
```

Step 3

Configure the BRI on SanJose1 and Capetown to use a dialer profile, as shown in the following:

Note: Do not assign an IP address to these interfaces.

```
SanJose1(config)#interface bri0/0
SanJose1(config-if)#isdn spid1 51055510000001 5551000
SanJose1(config-if)#isdn spid2 51055510010001 5551001
SanJose1(config-if)#encapsulation ppp
SanJose1(config-if)#ppp authentication chap
SanJose1(config-if)#dialer pool-member 1
SanJose1(config-if)#no shutdown

Capetown(config)#interface bri0/0
Capetown(config-if)#isdn spid1 51055520000001 5552000
Capetown(config-if)#isdn spid2 51055520010001 5552001
Capetown(config-if)#encapsulation ppp
Capetown(config-if)#ppp authentication chap
Capetown(config-if)#dialer pool-member 1
Capetown(config-if)#no shutdown
```

Dialer profiles were introduced in Cisco IOS version 11.2 and are the preferred way to configure DDR in complex environments. The dialer profile concept is based on a separation between logical and physical interface configuration. The use of dialer profiles allows the logical and physical configurations to be bound together dynamically on a per-call basis.

A dialer profile assigns an interface to a dialer pool or pools. In this case, BRI0/0 is assigned to dialer pool 1. The dialer interface assigns all the other logical configurations, such as IP address, dialer string, and dialer group. Depending on the IOS version, you might need to specify the line encapsulation on both the physical interface and the logical interface.

In Cisco IOS Software releases prior to IOS 12.0(7)T, dialer profiles in the same dialer pool need encapsulation configuration information. You must enter this information under both the dialer profile interface and the ISDN interface. If any conflict arises between the logical and the physical interfaces, the dialer profile does not work. That is why Step 4 shows this configuration with **encapsulation ppp** configured on BRI0/0 and dialer interface 0.

In the dynamic multiple encapsulations feature, in Cisco IOS 12.0(7)T and later, the new dialer profile model ignores the configuration on the ISDN interface. It uses only the configuration on the profile interface unless you use PPP name binding. Before a successful bind by calling line identification (CLID) occurs, no encapsulation type and configuration are assumed or taken from the physical interfaces.

Step 4

Configure the dialer interfaces for both routers, starting with SanJose1. The dialer interface receives the logical configuration that is applied to a physical interface. Issue the following commands on SanJose1:

```
SanJose1(config)#interface dialer 0
SanJose1(config-if)#dialer pool 1
SanJose1(config-if)#ip address 192.168.16.1 255.255.255.0
SanJose1(config-if)#encapsulation ppp
SanJose1(config-if)#ppp authentication chap
SanJose1(config-if)#ppp multilink
SanJose1(config-if)#dialer load-threshold 1 either
SanJose1(config-if)#dialer-group 1
SanJose1(config-if)#dialer remote-name Capetown
SanJose1(config-if)#dialer string 5552000
SanJose1(config-if)#dialer string 5552001
```

Now, create a dialer profile on Capetown, as shown in the following:

```
Capetown(config)#interface dialer 0
Capetown(config-if)#dialer pool 1
Capetown(config-if)#ip address 192.168.16.3 255.255.255.0
Capetown(config-if)#encapsulation ppp
Capetown(config-if)#ppp authentication chap
Capetown(config-if)#ppp multilink
Capetown(config-if)#dialer load-threshold 1 either
Capetown(config-if)#dialer-group 1
Capetown(config-if)#dialer remote-name SanJose1
Capetown(config-if)#dialer string 5551000
Capetown(config-if)#dialer string 5551001
```

Note: With a dialer interface, use the **dialer remote-name** and **dialer string** commands in place of a dialer map statement.

Use the **show isdn status** command to check ISDN Layer 2 and service profile identifier (SPID) status. Use the **clear interface bri0/0** command, multiple times if necessary, to enable a SPID status of established and valid.

1. How will SanJose1 know to use Capetown at 5552000 when it receives interesting traffic that must be routed to 192.168.16.3? In other words, is there anything in the dialer interface configuration that SanJose1 can use to determine that this dialer profile should be used to reach 192.168.16.3?

Step 5

Configure static routing on both routers so that nodes on the remote network can reach nodes at the central site. Use a default route on the Capetown router because it is a remote site stub network, as shown in the following:

```
SanJose1(config)#ip route 192.168.216.0 255.255.255.0 192.168.16.3
Capetown(config)#ip route 0.0.0.0 0.0.0.0 192.168.16.1
```

Step 6

Enable **debug dialer** on both SanJose1 and Capetown.

Test the ISDN connection by pinging Host B from Host A. This ping should eventually be successful. After you are connected, issue the **show dialer** command.

1.   According to the output from **show dialer**, what logical interface has been bound to interface BRI0/0:1?

_____

_____

Issue the **show ip interface brief** command. Because you configure PPP multilink, both B channels should show "up and up." Troubleshoot as necessary.

Allow the ISDN connection to time out, or manually disconnect both B channels by issuing the **isdn test disconnect interface bri0/0 all** command at either router.

With both B channels disconnected on each router, issue the **show ip interface brief** command a second time.

2.   According to this command, interface Dialer0 is still "up and up." Why?

_____

_____

Lab 5.3.2: Using a Dialer Map Class with Dialer Profiles

Estimated Time: 45 Minutes

Objective

In this lab, you configure two Cisco routers for ISDN BRI using dialer profiles and a dialer map class. Figure 5-2 shows the sample topology.

Figure 5-2   Sample Topology for Lab 5.3.2

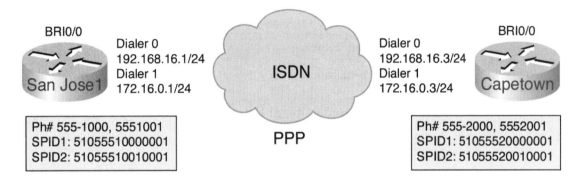

Equipment Requirements

This lab requires an Adtran Atlas 550 or similar device and 2600 or 1700 series routers, as shown in Figure 5-2.

Scenario

The International Travel Agency wants you to configure an ISDN DDR connection between the corporate network router, SanJose1, and its remote office router in Capetown. It has asked that you configure PPP encapsulation and CHAP authentication over this link. Because the company plans to increase the number of ISDN connections at the central and remote sites, use dialer profiles to simplify future configurations.

The company has only one remote site connection at this time. However, you configure two dialer profiles to test its operation. Because you test router-to-router connectivity, you do not need to configure the workstations in this lab.

Step 1

Before beginning this lab, reload the router after erasing its startup configuration. This step prevents problems that residual configurations might cause. Build the network according to Figure 5-2, but do not configure the BRI interfaces on either router yet. Use the Adtran Atlas 550 or a similar device to simulate the ISDN cloud. If you use the Atlas 550, be sure to use straight-through cables. Connect both routers to the BRI module ports of the Atlas 550, as labeled in Figure 5-2.

Step 2

Configure both routers to use the appropriate ISDN switch type, National ISDN-1. You use PPP encapsulation and CHAP on the B channels. For this reason, enter the case-sensitive username and password information on both routers. Notice in the following that this lab uses different passwords and username combinations than previous labs did:

```
SanJose1(config)#isdn switch-type basic-ni
SanJose1(config)#username Capetown password cisco
SanJose1(config)#username JULIET password cisco
SanJose1(config)#enable password cisco
SanJose1(config)#line vty 0 4
SanJose1(config-line)#password cisco
SanJose1(config-line)#login

Capetown(config)#isdn switch-type basic-ni
Capetown(config)#username SanJose1 password cisco
Capetown(config)#username ROMEO password cisco
Capetown(config)#enable password cisco
Capetown(config)#line vty 0 4
Capetown(config-line)#password cisco
Capetown(config-line)#login
```

Configure **dialer-list 5** on both routers to identify all IP traffic as interesting. The following is an example for SanJose1:

```
SanJose1(config)#dialer-list 5 protocol ip permit
```

Step 3

Configure the BRI on SanJose1 and Capetown to use dialer profiles. In this lab, configure both BRIs to be members of a dialer pool as follows:

```
SanJose1(config)#interface bri0/0
SanJose1(config-if)#isdn spid1 51055510000001 5551000
SanJose1(config-if)#isdn spid2 51055510010001 5551001
SanJose1(config-if)#encapsulation ppp
SanJose1(config-if)#ppp authentication chap
SanJose1(config-if)#dialer pool-member 1
SanJose1(config-if)#no shutdown

Capetown(config)#interface bri0/0
Capetown(config-if)#isdn spid1 51055520000001 5552000
Capetown(config-if)#isdn spid2 51055520010001 5552001
Capetown(config-if)#encapsulation ppp
Capetown(config-if)#ppp authentication chap
Capetown(config-if)#dialer pool-member 1
Capetown(config-if)#no shutdown
```

Note: Remember that you must enter the encapsulation configuration commands for both the physical interface, BRI 0/0, and the logical interface, such as Dialer0.

Step 4

On both routers, create a map class called AGGRESSIVE that you can use to apply multiple dialer configurations to a dialer string easily. Issue the following commands on both routers. The following is an example for SanJose1:

```
SanJose1(config)#map-class dialer AGGRESSIVE
SanJose1(config-map-class)#dialer idle-timeout 30
SanJose1(config-map-class)#dialer fast-idle 10
SanJose1(config-map-class)#dialer wait-for-carrier-time 25
SanJose1(config-map-class)#exit
```

1.   Other than a dialer map class, what other types of map classes can you configure?

_____

_____

Note: Use the help feature to find the answer.

Step 5

Configure the dialer interfaces for both routers as follows, starting with SanJose1:

```
SanJose1(config)#interface dialer 0
SanJose1(config-if)#ip address 192.168.16.1 255.255.255.0
SanJose1(config-if)#dialer pool 1
SanJose1(config-if)#encapsulation ppp
SanJose1(config-if)#ppp authentication chap
SanJose1(config-if)#dialer remote-name Capetown
SanJose1(config-if)#dialer-group 5
SanJose1(config-if)#dialer string 5552000 class AGGRESSIVE
SanJose1(config-if)#dialer string 5552001 class AGGRESSIVE

SanJose1(config)#interface dialer 1
SanJose1(config-if)#ip address 172.16.0.1 255.255.255.0
SanJose1(config-if)#dialer pool 1
SanJose1(config-if)#encapsulation ppp
SanJose1(config-if)#ppp authentication chap
SanJose1(config-if)#ppp chap hostname ROMEO
SanJose1(config-if)#dialer remote-name JULIET
SanJose1(config-if)#dialer-group 5
SanJose1(config-if)#dialer string 5552000 class AGGRESSIVE
SanJose1(config-if)#dialer string 5552001 class AGGRESSIVE
```

Note: The dialer interface receives the logical configuration that is applied to a physical interface.

1.   When you apply the map class AGGRESSIVE to each dialer string, which timers are being configured?

_____

_____

2.   What does the command **ppp chap hostname ROMEO** do?

_____

_____

Now create the dialer profiles on Capetown, as shown in the following:

```
Capetown(config)#interface dialer 0
Capetown(config-if)#ip address 192.168.16.3 255.255.255.0
Capetown(config-if)#dialer pool 1
Capetown(config-if)#encapsulation ppp
Capetown(config-if)#ppp authentication chap
Capetown(config-if)#dialer remote-name SanJose1
Capetown(config-if)#dialer-group 5
Capetown(config-if)#dialer string 5551000 class AGGRESSIVE
Capetown(config-if)#dialer string 5551001 class AGGRESSIVE

Capetown(config)#interface dialer 1
Capetown(config-if)#ip address 172.16.0.3 255.255.255.0
Capetown(config-if)#dialer pool 1
```

```
Capetown(config-if)#encapsulation ppp
Capetown(config-if)#ppp authentication chap
Capetown(config-if)#ppp chap hostname JULIET
Capetown(config-if)#dialer remote-name ROMEO
Capetown(config-if)#dialer-group 5
Capetown(config-if)#dialer string 5551000 class AGGRESSIVE
Capetown(config-if)#dialer string 5551001 class AGGRESSIVE
```

Step 6

To simplify testing, create host-name mappings on both routers:

```
SanJose1(config)#ip host Capetown 192.168.16.3
SanJose1(config)#ip host JULIET 172.16.0.3

Capetown(config)#ip host SanJose1 192.168.16.1
Capetown(config)#ip host ROMEO 172.16.0.1
```

Note: Make sure that the host names configured here exactly match the previously configured CHAP and dialer remote host names.

Step 7

Before connecting, issue the **show dialer** command.

1.   According to the output of this command, what is the dialer idle timeout for BRI0/0:1 set to?

_____

_____

2.   What is the fast idle timer for BRI0/0:1 set to?

_____

_____

Use the **show isdn status** command on both routers to check the ISDN Layer 2 and SPID status. Use the **clear interface bri0/0** command, multiple times if necessary, to enable a SPID status of established and valid.

Now, test the dialer profile operation. Enter the **debug dialer** and **debug ppp authentication** commands. Use the following command to **ping** Capetown, 192.168.16.3, from SanJose1:

```
SanJose1#ping Capetown
```

SanJose1 should dial Capetown and connect. The pings should eventually be successful, as the following shows:

```
Type escape sequence to abort.
Sending 5, 100-byte ICMP Echos to 192.168.16.3, timeout is 2 seconds:

14:36:24: BR0/0 DDR: rotor dialout [priority]
14:36:24: BR0/0 DDR: Dialing cause ip (s=192.168.16.1, d=192.168.16.3)
14:36:24: BR0/0 DDR: Attempting to dial 5552000
14:36:24: %LINK-3-UPDOWN: Interface BRI0/0:1, changed state to up
14:36:24: BR0/0:1: interface must be fifo queue, force fifo
14:36:24: %DIALER-6-BIND: Interface BR0/0:1 bound to profile Di0
14:36:24: BR0/0:1 PPP: Using dialer call direction
14:36:24: BR0/0:1 PPP: Treating connection as a callout
14:36:24: BR0/0:1 CHAP: O CHALLENGE id 1 len 29 from "SanJose1"
```

```
14:36:24: BR0/0:1 AUTH: Started process 0 pid 106
14:36:24: BR0/0:1 CHAP: I CHALLENGE id 1 len 29 from "Capetown"
14:36:24: BR0/0:1 CHAP: O RESPONSE id 1 len 29 from "SanJose1"
14:36:24: BR0/0:1 CHAP: I SUCCESS id 1 len 4
14:36:24: BR0/0:1 CHAP: I RESPONSE id 1 len 29 from "Capetown"
14:36:24: BR0/0:1 CHAP: O SUCCESS id 1 len 4
14:36:24: BR0/0:1 DDR: dialer protocol up.!!!!
Success rate is 80 percent (4/5), round-trip min/avg/max = 32/33/36 ms
```

3.　According to the output of the **debug dialer** command, what logical interface is bound to interface BRI0/0:1?

Troubleshoot as necessary. With SanJose1 still connected to Capetown, reconnect if necessary and **ping** JULIET from SanJose1 using the following command:

```
SanJose1#ping JULIET
```

Again, the connection and pings should eventually be successful, using the second B channel, BRI0/0:2. Troubleshoot as necessary. Be sure to ping JULIET while the connection to Capetown is still in use. If the connection to Capetown times out, BRI0/0:1 is used again because it is available.

4.　According to the output of the **debug dialer** command, what logical interface is bound to interface BRI0/0:2?

With both connections still active, issue the **show dialer** command on SanJose1. A partial sample output follows:

```
SanJose1#show dialer
********output omitted********
BRI0/0:1 - dialer type = ISDN
Idle timer (30 secs), Fast idle timer (10 secs)
Wait for carrier (25 secs), Re-enable (15 secs)
Dialer state is data link layer up
Dial reason: ip (s=192.168.16.1, d=192.168.16.3)
Interface bound to profile Dialer0
Time until disconnect 4 secs
Current call connected 00:00:29
Connected to 5552000 (Capetown)

BRI0/0:2 - dialer type = ISDN
Idle timer (30 secs), Fast idle timer (10 secs)
Wait for carrier (25 secs), Re-enable (15 secs)
Dialer state is data link layer up
Dial reason: ip (s=172.16.0.1, d=172.16.0.3)
Interface bound to profile Dialer1
Time until disconnect 19 secs
Current call connected 00:00:13
Connected to 5552001 (JULIET)


Dialer0 - dialer type = DIALER PROFILE
Idle timer (120 secs), Fast idle timer (20 secs)
Wait for carrier (30 secs), Re-enable (15 secs)
Dialer state is data link layer up
```

```
Number of active calls = 0
Number of active circuit switched calls = 0
*******output omitted*******
```

5. According to the output of the **show dialer** command, what phone number is BRI0/0:1 connected to? What is the host name of that router?

_____

_____

6. What phone number is BRI0/0:2 connected to? What is the host name of that router?

_____

7. According to the output of the **show dialer** command, what is the idle timer for BRI0/0:1 set to?

_____

_____

8. What is the fast idle timer for BRI0/0:1 set to?

_____

_____

9. Why did these values change when SanJose1 connected to Capetown?

_____

_____

_____

10. What is one advantage of using a dialer profile instead of a dedicated configuration on the BRI?

_____

_____

_____

_____

11. What is one advantage of using a dialer map class?

_____

_____

_____

_____

Chapter 6

Frame Relay

Lab 6.4.1: Basic Frame Relay Router and Switch Configuration

Estimated Time: 45 Minutes

Objective

In this lab, you configure a router as a Frame Relay switch, connecting two routers in a point-to-point topology. Figure 6-1 shows the sample topology you use.

Figure 6-1   Sample Topology for Lab 6.4.1

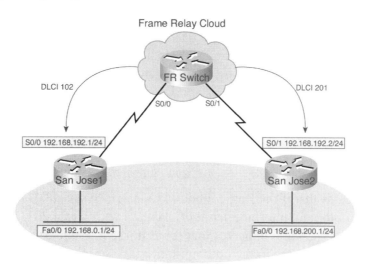

Equipment Requirements

This lab requires 2600 or 1700 series routers.

Scenario

As the network engineer for International Travel Agency, prepare to deploy Frame Relay as the primary connectivity for the company WAN. While waiting for the service provider to provision T1 lines, create router configurations in advance. Because access to a Frame Relay switch is not available, you must configure a Cisco router as a Frame Relay switch to test router configurations. This network uses Interior Gateway Routing Protocol (IGRP), autonomous system number 234, to advertise LANs at each location.

Step 1

Before beginning this lab, you should reload each router after erasing its startup configuration. Taking this step prevents problems that residual configurations might cause. After you prepare the equipment, proceed with Step 2. Configure each router with its respective host name and Fast Ethernet IP addresses and connect the Fast Ethernet interface to a switch or a hub.

Step 2

Configure the Frame Relay switch with static mapping necessary to switch packets along the appropriate permanent virtual circuit (PVC).

Enable **frame-relay switching** on the router acting as the service provider Frame Relay cloud as follows:

```
FRswitch(config)#frame-relay switching
```

The remaining configurations on the Frame Relay switch are specific to the interfaces. On each serial interface, configure the encapsulation to Frame Relay, define the interface as a Frame Relay DCE (data communications equipment), and set the clockrate. The following is an example:

```
FRswitch(config-if)#encapsulation frame-relay
FRswitch(config-if)#frame-relay intf-type dce
FRswitch(config-if)#clock rate 56000
```

Frame Relay switches identify inbound frames by their data-link connection identifier (DLCI). The DLCI is then referenced in a switching table to determine the outbound port. Statically define an end-to-end PVC between SanJose1 and London. You need to configure a static route for each serial interface, as shown in the following:

```
FRswitch(config)#interface serial 0/0
FRswitch(config-if)#frame-relay route 102 interface serial 0/1 201
FRswitch(config-if)#interface serial 0/1
FRswitch(config-if)#frame-relay route 201 interface serial 0/0 102
```

The switch logic indicates that if the frame inbound to interface serial 0/0 is labeled DLCI 102, send the frame to the outbound interface serial 0/1 labeled with DLCI 201. For traffic traveling in the opposite direction, the logic indicates that if the frame inbound to interface serial 0/1 is labeled DLCI 201, send the frame to the outbound interface serial 0/0 labeled with DLCI 102. You can confirm this arrangement with the **show frame-relay route** on the switch, as shown in the following:

```
FRswitch#show frame-relay route
Input Intf     Input Dlci      Output Intf     Output Dlci     Status
Serial0/0      102              Serial0/1       201             active
Serial0/1      201              Serial0/0       102             active
```

Step 3

Next, configure SanJose1 with IP addresses and a routing protocol, as shown in Figure 6-1. The default encapsulation for Cisco routers is High-Level Data Link Control (HDLC). Therefore, you must configure the interface serial 0/0 for Frame Relay encapsulation, as the following shows:

```
SanJose1(config)#interface serial 0/0
SanJose1(config-if)#encapsulation frame-relay
SanJose1(config-if)#ip address 192.168.192.1 255.255.255.0
SanJose1(config-if)#exit
SanJose1(config)#router igrp 234
SanJose1(config-router)#network 192.168.0.0
SanJose1(config-router)#network 192.168.192.0
```

Configure London using the same command syntax.

Step 4

Use extended pings and **show ip route** to test Frame Relay connectivity and IGRP route propagation as follows:

```
London#show ip route
Gateway of last resort is not set
C    192.168.192.0/24 is directly connected, Serial0/0
C    192.168.200.0/24 is directly connected, FastEthernet0/0
I    192.168.0.0/24 [100/80135] via 192.168.192.1, 00:00:25,
Serial0/0


London#ping
Protocol [ip]:
Target IP address: 192.168.0.1
Repeat count [5]: 20
Datagram size [100]:
Timeout in seconds [2]:
Extended commands [n]: y
Source address or interface: 192.168.200.1
Type of service [0]:
Set DF bit in IP header? [no]:
Validate reply data? [no]:
Data pattern [0xABCD]:
Loose, Strict, Record, Timestamp, Verbose[none]:
Sweep range of sizes [n]:
Type escape sequence to abort.
Sending 20, 100-byte ICMP Echos to 192.168.0.1, timeout is 2
seconds:
!!!!!!!!!!!!!!!!!!!!!
Success rate is 100 percent (20/20), round-trip min/avg/max = 64/64/68 ms
```

That is the total process to configure an end-to-end Frame Relay network. It is a simple process because Cisco routers can dynamically learn information from the adjacent Frame Relay switch and neighboring routers.

Step 5

Many variables are defined through default configuration and discovery. However, you can still display those default values, such as Frame Relay encapsulation type, DLCI mapping, and Local Management Interface (LMI).

Cisco routers support two Frame Relay encapsulation types: Cisco and Internet Engineering Task Force (IETF). Cisco is a proprietary encapsulation type; IETF is standards based. Use IETF whenever connecting to a non–Cisco router through a Frame Relay PVC. Because you have not defined the Frame Relay encapsulation type, the default must be in use. Issue the **show interface serial 0/0** command as follows, on SanJose1:

```
SanJose1#show interface serial 0/0
Serial0/0 is up, line protocol is up
  Hardware is PowerQUICC Serial
  Internet address is 192.168.192.1/24
  MTU 1500 bytes, BW 1544 Kbit, DLY 20000 usec,
     reliability 255/255, txload 1/255, rxload 1/255
  Encapsulation FRAME-RELAY, loopback not set
  Keepalive set (10 sec)
!
*******output omitted*******
```

In the previous output, there is no indication of the encapsulation type other than FRAME-RELAY. Change SanJose1 Serial 0/0 Frame Relay encapsulation type to IETF, as follows:

```
SanJose1(config)#interface serial 0/0
SanJose1(config-if)#encapsulation frame-relay ietf
```

Now, enter the **show interface serial 0/0** command again:

```
SanJose1#show interface serial 0/0
Serial0/0 is up, line protocol is up
Hardware is PowerQUICC Serial
Internet address is 192.168.192.1/24
MTU 1500 bytes, BW 1544 Kbit, DLY 20000 usec,
reliability 255/255, txload 1/255, rxload 1/255
Encapsulation FRAME-RELAY IETF, loopback not set
Keepalive set (10 sec)
!
*******output omitted*******
```

The preceding output declares the IETF encapsulation type. When you see only FRAME-RELAY, the router is using the default encapsulation type, Cisco. Change the encapsulation type back to Cisco by not specifying a type:

```
SanJose1(config)#interface serial 0/0
SanJose1(config-if)#encapsulation frame-relay
```

DLCIs identify unique PVCs or switched virtual circuits (SVCs). One device can support DLCIs ranging from 16 to 1007. The complete DLCI range is 0 to 1023, with 0 to 15 and 1008 to 1023 reserved for special purposes. For example, multicasts are identified with 1019 and 1020.

Issue the **show frame-relay map** command as follows on SanJose1:

```
SanJose1#show frame-relay map
Serial0/0 (up): ip 192.168.192.2 dlci 102(0x12,0x420), dynamic,
                broadcast,, status defined, active
```

The association between a DLCI and its next-hop network address is called *mapping*. The router logic indicates that if routing to the next-hop address 192.168.192.2, then tag the frame with DLCI 102. The Frame Relay switch does not understand IP addressing but does know where to send frames tagged as DLCI 102. Recall the switch logic from Step 2.

1. Given the minimal commands executed on SanJose1, how does the router know which DLCI to use? How does the router know the IP address of the next-hop router using that PVC?

    _____

    _____

    _____

    _____

You must configure DLCIs on the Frame Relay switch. If you do not configure DLCIs on the router, they are learned dynamically from the switch through LMI as defined in the next paragraph. Once the router has a DLCI number identifying a virtual circuit, the router sends an Inverse Address Resolution Protocol (ARP) through that circuit, requesting information from whatever DTE is on the other end. When the process is completed in both directions, the circuit is ready for traffic.

LMI is the Layer 2 protocol between the router (DTE) and the Frame Relay switch (DCE). LMI exchanges keepalives every 10 seconds, with DLCI information conveyed every 60 seconds. There are three different LMI types:

- Cisco

- ANSI

- Q933a

DTE devices must match the LMI type of the DCE. Because you did not explicitly configure the LMI type on the Frame Relay switch, the network must be using the default LMI type. Execute the **show frame-relay lmi** command as follows on SanJose1:

```
SanJose1#show frame-relay lmi
LMI Statistics for interface Serial0/0 (Frame Relay DTE) LMI TYPE = CISCO
  Invalid Unnumbered info 0        Invalid Prot Disc 0
  Invalid dummy Call Ref 0         Invalid Msg Type 0
  Invalid Status Message 0         Invalid Lock Shift 0
  Invalid Information ID 0         Invalid Report IE Len 0
  Invalid Report Request 0         Invalid Keep IE Len 0
  Num Status Enq. Sent 325         Num Status msgs Rcvd 326
  Num Update Status Rcvd 0         Num Status Timeouts 0
```

The default LMI type is Cisco. Notice that LMI type is interface-specific. This same router could use a different LMI type on another serial interface. It might do so when connected to a second Frame Relay switch for redundancy. The LMI type is also identified by a DLCI, communicated from the switch to the router.

2.   Which DLCI does the Cisco LMI type use?

If you do not already know the answer, issue the **show interface serial 0/0** command as follows on SanJose1:

```
SanJose1#show interface serial 0/0
Serial0/0 is up, line protocol is up
  Hardware is PowerQUICC Serial
  Internet address is 192.168.192.1/24
  MTU 1500 bytes, BW 1544 Kbit, DLY 20000 usec,
     reliability 255/255, txload 1/255, rxload 1/255
  Encapsulation FRAME-RELAY, loopback not set
  Keepalive set (10 sec)
  LMI enq sent  109, LMI stat recvd 109, LMI upd recvd 0, DTE
     LMI up
  LMI enq recvd 0, LMI stat sent  0, LMI upd sent  0
  LMI DLCI 1023  LMI type is CISCO  frame relay DTE
  Broadcast queue 0/64, broadcasts sent/dropped 36/0, interface
broadcasts 17
  Last input 00:00:05, output 00:00:05, output hang never
  Last clearing of "show interface" counters 00:18:15
!
********output omitted********
```

The Cisco LMI type is using DLCI 1023.

You can implement Frame Relay in four basic topologies:

- Point-to-point

- Hub and spoke (star)

- Full mesh

- Partial mesh

Frame Relay is easy to configure in a simple topology, but it has many variations. Complication is introduced when multiple PVCs share one physical interface or when you implement a nonbroadcast multiaccess network (NBMA) over Frame Relay. The following labs address common variations.

Lab 6.4.2: Configuring Full-Mesh Frame Relay

Estimated Time: 30 Minutes

Objective

In this lab, you configure three routers with Frame Relay in a full-mesh topology. Figure 6-2 shows the sample topology you use.

Figure 6-2   Sample Topology for Lab 6.4.2

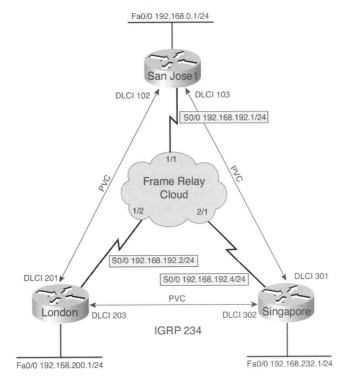

Equipment Requirements

This lab requires Adtran Atlas 550 or a similar device and 2600 or 1700 series routers.

Scenario

The Internet service provider (ISP) has provisioned Frame Relay PVCs for the International Travel Agency WAN. You have the responsibility of configuring Frame Relay between offices located in North America, Asia, and Europe. The design calls for you to place all three routers on the same logical IP network in a full-mesh topology. Also, use IGRP (AS 234) to dynamically exchange routes. The ISP Frame Relay switch uses the ANSI LMI-type and is configured with the DLCIs displayed in Figure 6-2.

Step 1

Before beginning this lab, reload each router after erasing its startup configuration. This step prevents problems that residual configurations can cause. After you prepare the equipment, proceed with Step 2. Cable the network according to Figure 6-2. This lab assumes that you use an Adtran Atlas 550 to emulate the Frame Relay cloud. You can also use a router with three serial interfaces as a Frame Relay switch. If you use the Atlas 550, be sure to connect the serial interfaces on the router to the port on the Atlas using a V.35 cable, as labeled in the diagram.

Even if you use a WAN emulator, perform the lab both ways if possible. Being able to configure a router as a Frame Relay switch in a full-mesh topology is beneficial to understanding Frame Relay connectivity.

Step 2

On SanJose1, apply IP addressing to the interfaces. Configure IGRP as the routing protocol and encapsulate the Serial 0/0 WAN link as Frame Relay, as shown in the following:

```
SanJose1(config)#interface serial 0/0
SanJose1(config-if)#ip address 192.168.192.1 255.255.255.0
SanJose1(config-if)#encapsulation frame-relay
SanJose1(config-if)#interface fastethernet 0/0
SanJose1(config-if)#ip address 192.168.0.1 255.255.255.0
SanJose1(config-if)#exit
SanJose1(config)#router igrp 234
SanJose1(config-router)#network 192.168.0.0
SanJose1(config-router)#network 192.168.192.0
```

Configure Frame Relay on Singapore and London using the same command syntax.

Step 3

Verify the complete configuration of the full-mesh Frame Relay WAN.

Verify router connectivity using extended pings between Fast Ethernet interfaces. Do not ping the Frame Relay serial interfaces because they will not reply. The following is an extended ping example between London and Singapore:

```
London#ping
Protocol [ip]:
Target IP address: 192.168.232.1
Repeat count [5]: 50
Datagram size [100]:
Timeout in seconds [2]:
Extended commands [n]: y
Source address or interface: 192.168.200.1
Type of service [0]:
Set DF bit in IP header? [no]:
Validate reply data? [no]:
Data pattern [0xABCD]:
Loose, Strict, Record, Timestamp, Verbose[none]:
Sweep range of sizes [n]:
Type escape sequence to abort.
Sending 50, 100-byte ICMP Echos to 192.168.232.1, timeout is 2
seconds:
!!!!!!!!!!!!!!!!!!!!!!!!!!!!!!!!!!!!!!!!!!!!!!!!!!!
Success rate is 100 percent (50/50), round-trip min/avg/max = 56/60/80 ms
```

All pings should be successful. With only one physical connection to the Frame Relay cloud, you can reach two different next-hop routers.

Issue the **show frame-relay lmi** command on Singapore. Output should be similar to the following:

```
Singapore#show frame-relay lmi
LMI Statistics for interface Serial0/0 (Frame Relay DTE) LMI TYPE = ANSI
  Invalid Unnumbered info 0          Invalid Prot Disc 0
  Invalid dummy Call Ref 0           Invalid Msg Type 0
  Invalid Status Message 0           Invalid Lock Shift 0
  Invalid Information ID 0           Invalid Report IE Len 0
  Invalid Report Request 0           Invalid Keep IE Len 0
```

```
Num Status Enq. Sent 2523          Num Status msgs Rcvd 2522
Num Update Status Rcvd 0           Num Status Timeouts 7
The LMI type is ANSI.
```

1. On Cisco routers, the default LMI type is Cisco. However, LMI type ANSI was selected but not explicitly configured. Why did the router select ANSI?

_____

_____

_____

_____

If a router is running Cisco IOS release 11.2 or later, it can autosense the LMI type as either Cisco, ANSI T1.617 Annex D (ANSI), or ITU-T Q.933 Annex A (q933a).

Issue the **show frame-relay pvc** command as follows on Singapore:

```
Singapore#show frame-relay pvc
PVC Statistics for interface Serial0/0 (Frame Relay DTE)
              Active        Inactive       Deleted        Static
  Local         2              0              0              0
  Switched      0              0              0              0
  Unused        0              0              0              0
DLCI = 301, DLCI USAGE = LOCAL, PVC STATUS = ACTIVE, INTERFACE = Serial0/0
  input pkts 676          output pkts 470          in bytes 92211
  out bytes 86466         dropped pkts 0           in FECN pkts 0
  in BECN pkts 0          out FECN pkts 0          out BECN pkts 0
  in DE pkts 0            out DE pkts 0
  out bcast pkts 372       out bcast bytes 76274
  pvc create time 03:32:04, last time pvc status changed 03:32:04
DLCI = 302, DLCI USAGE = LOCAL, PVC STATUS = ACTIVE, INTERFACE = Serial0/0
  input pkts 433          output pkts 436          in bytes 81309
  out bytes 82942         dropped pkts 0           in FECN pkts 0
  in BECN pkts 0          out FECN pkts 0          out BECN pkts 0
  in DE pkts 0            out DE pkts 0
  out bcast pkts 371       out bcast bytes 76182
  pvc create time 03:32:05, last time pvc status changed 03:32:05
```

Singapore S0/0 is using DLCI 301 and 302. They were not explicitly configured. The router dynamically learned about the DLCIs from the Frame Relay switch. Recall that a DLCI identifies the PVCs through the Frame Relay cloud.

Issue the **show frame-relay map** command as follows on Singapore:

```
Singapore#show frame-relay map
Serial0/0 (up): ip 192.168.192.1 dlci 301(0x10,0x400), dynamic,
           broadcast,, status defined, active
Serial0/0 (up): ip 192.168.192.2 dlci 302(0x11,0x410), dynamic,
           broadcast,, status defined, active
```

Recall that mapping is the association between a DLCI and the next-hop DTE router. The next hop is identified by its IP address.

2. You did not explicitly configure mapping, so how was this mapping achieved?

_____

Once a router receives a list of DLCIs, it sends an Inverse ARP through every identified PVC. The Inverse ARP requests information regarding the DTE at the other end. The map table displays the returned IP address and status information. According to the **show frame-relay map** command output, these maps were created dynamically.

Note: Broadcasts and multicasts are supported on these PVCs, enabling routing protocols to exchange updates between regional sites.

Now, issue the **show ip route** command as follows on Singapore:

```
Singapore#show ip route
Gateway of last resort is not set
C    192.168.192.0/24 is directly connected, Serial0/0
I    192.168.200.0/24 [100/8486] via 192.168.192.2, 00:00:03, Serial0/0
C    192.168.232.0/24 is directly connected, FastEthernet0/0
I    192.168.0.0/24 [100/8486] via 192.168.192.1, 00:00:05, Serial0/0
```

Singapore should have a complete routing table, indicating that the full-mesh Frame Relay configuration is complete. If the routing table is not complete, perhaps IGRP has not yet converged.

Step 4

Network engineers might not be comfortable with implicit configurations. The benefits of dynamic mapping are minor due to the static nature of most WANs. After a link is established, there might not be a change for years. Also, if you do not explicitly define variables with configuration commands, the configuration file does not yield much information about the Frame Relay network.

You can explicitly configure the routers to define the elements discussed previously. The following is an example of how you could manually configure SanJose1:

```
SanJose1(config)#interface fastethernet 0/0
SanJose1(config-if)#ip address 192.168.0.1 255.255.255.0
SanJose1(config-if)#interface serial 0/0
SanJose1(config-if)#encapsulation frame-relay
SanJose1(config-if)#frame-relay map ip 192.168.192.2 102 broadcast
SanJose1(config-if)#frame-relay map ip 192.168.192.4 103 broadcast
SanJose1(config-if)#frame-relay lmi-type ansi
SanJose1(config-if)#exit
SanJose1(config)#router igrp 234
SanJose1(config-router)#network 192.168.192.0
SanJose1(config-router)#network 192.168.0.0
SanJose1(config-router)#passive-interface fastethernet 0/0
```

The **frame-relay map** command associates next-hop IP addresses with a local DLCI. The **broadcast** keyword allows multicasts and broadcasts to be propagated through that PVC. The **frame-relay lmi-type** command statically defines the DTE (router) LMI protocol, which must match the DCE (Frame Relay switch).

Notice that in this configuration, IGRP routing updates are blocked from exiting Fast Ethernet 0/0. This setup saves bandwidth on the LAN because there are no IGRP neighbors on that network.

Lab 6.4.3: Configuring Full-Mesh Frame Relay with Subinterfaces

Estimated Time: 30 Minutes

Objective

In this lab, you configure three routers with Frame Relay in a full mesh using subinterfaces. Figure 6-3 shows the sample topology you use.

Figure 6-3   Sample Topology for Lab 6.4.3

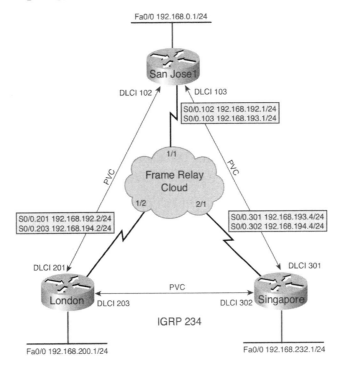

Equipment Requirements

This lab requires an Adtran Atlas 550 or similar device and 2600 or 1700 series routers.

Scenario

Rather than fine-tune traffic flow among regional sites connected to the International Travel Agency WAN, you could implement greater control if there was an individual physical leased line between each site. Unfortunately, the cost of an additional leased line is not approved.

However, by using subinterfaces, you can configure separate logical connections between the sites. Each router has one physical interface connected to the Frame Relay switch. To allow each router to reach the other sites, you must configure two logical subinterfaces for the single physical interface (s0/0). Physical redundancy is achieved in the carrier's Frame Relay cloud. You use multiple PVCs for each physical interface on the routers. Although the service provider charges for each additional PVC, the fee is typically less than the cost of a leased line.

Step 1

Before beginning this lab, you should reload each router after erasing its startup configuration. This step prevents problems that residual configurations can cause. After you prepare the equipment, proceed with Step 2.

Build the network according to Figure 6-3. This lab assumes that you use an Adtran Atlas 550 to emulate the Frame Relay cloud. You can also use other WAN emulators or a router as a Frame Relay switch. If you use the Atlas 550, be sure to connect the serial interface of each router to the port on the Atlas using a V.35 cable, as labeled in the figure.

Step 2

Configure the Fast Ethernet interface and IGRP (AS 234) on each router as shown in Figure 6-3. Configure serial interfaces to use Frame Relay with subinterfaces. Enter the following commands on SanJose1:

```
SanJose1(config)#interface serial 0/0
SanJose1(config-if)#encapsulation frame-relay
SanJose1(config-if)#frame-relay lmi-type ansi
SanJose1(config-if)#no shutdown
```

You do not need to configure this interface with an IP address. The IP addresses are assigned to each subinterface.

You can enter Frame Relay interfaces as either point-to-point or multipoint configurations. Some versions of Cisco IOS let you create a subinterface without specifying either type. This choice results in a multipoint subinterface, which is the default.

In this scenario, you configure a point-to-point subinterface using DLCI 103. A common practice is to the number the subinterface by referencing its DLCI number. This numbering makes it easier to determine which PVC each subinterface it is using. For example, subinterface 0.103 uses DLCI 103.

Configure the DLCI 103 subinterface with the keyword **point-to-point**, as shown in the following:

```
SanJose1(config)#interface s0/0.103 point-to-point
SanJose1(config-subif)#ip address 192.168.193.1 255.255.255.0
SanJose1(config-subif)#frame-relay interface-dlci 103
```

You use the **frame-relay interface-dlci** command to specify which DLCI is used by each subinterface. Point-to-point subinterfaces can each use only one DLCI. If you do not specify a subinterface for a DLCI, it is associated with its major interface (for example, s0/0).

Configure the DLCI 102 subinterface as follows:

```
SanJose1(config)#interface s0/0.102 point-to-point
SanJose1(config-subif)#ip address 192.168.192.1 255.255.255.0
SanJose1(config-subif)#frame-relay interface-dlci 102
```

Configure London and Singapore according to Figure 6-3. Use the command syntax in this step as a guide.

Step 3

Verify PVC status by issuing the following **show frame-relay pvc** command on SanJose1:

```
SanJose1#show frame-relay pvc
PVC Statistics for interface Serial0/0 (Frame Relay DTE)
                Active      Inactive      Deleted      Static
  Local           2             1            0            0
  Switched        0             0            0            0
  Unused          0             0            0            0
```

```
DLCI = 104, DLCI USAGE = LOCAL, PVC STATUS = INACTIVE, INTERFACE = Serial0/0
  input pkts 0              output pkts 0          in bytes 0
  out bytes 0              dropped pkts 0          in FECN pkts 0
  in BECN pkts 0           out FECN pkts 0         out BECN pkts 0
  in DE pkts 0             out DE pkts 0
  out bcast pkts 0          out bcast bytes 0
  pvc create time 00:48:21, last time pvc status changed 00:48:21

DLCI = 103, DLCI USAGE = LOCAL, PVC STATUS = ACTIVE, INTERFACE
  = Serial0/0.103
  input pkts 167           output pkts 179         in bytes 21552
  out bytes 19871          dropped pkts 5          in FECN pkts 0
  in BECN pkts 0           out FECN pkts 0         out BECN pkts 0
  in DE pkts 0             out DE pkts 0
  out bcast pkts 59         out bcast bytes 10890
  pvc create time 00:48:34, last time pvc status changed 00:29:13

DLCI = 102, DLCI USAGE = LOCAL, PVC STATUS = ACTIVE, INTERFACE =
  Serial0/0.102
  input pkts 156           output pkts 135         in bytes 27757
  out bytes 18758          dropped pkts 5          in FECN pkts 0
  in BECN pkts 0           out FECN pkts 0         out BECN pkts 0
  in DE pkts 0             out DE pkts 0
  out bcast pkts 55         out bcast bytes 10718
  pvc create time 00:48:35, last time pvc status changed 00:07:14
```

The output of the **show frame-relay pvc** command shows how the router perceives the PVC status. The different states are ACTIVE, INACTIVE, and DELETED. ACTIVE is a successful end-to-end (DTE to DTE) circuit. INACTIVE is a successful connection to the Frame Relay switch (DTE to DCE) without a DTE detected on the other end of the PVC. This state can occur if the router dynamically learns of a DLCI not intended for its network. There might be a residual or incorrect configuration on the Frame Relay switch. The DELETED state is when the DTE is configured for a DLCI the switch does not recognize as valid for that interface.

If you see any INACTIVE DLCIs that are not to be used, check with the service provider regarding their status. In this configuration, SanJose1 detects DLCI 104, which this lab does not use. To keep the router from dynamically creating a PVC with whatever DTE is on the other end, disable Inverse ARP for DLCI 104, as shown in the following:

```
SanJose1(config)#interface serial 0/0
SanJose1(config-if)#no frame-relay inverse-arp ip 104
```

Issue the **show frame-relay map** command on SanJose1 to determine whether Frame Relay mapped the appropriate DLCIs to the correct IP address:

```
SanJose1#show frame-relay map
Serial0/0.103 (up): point-to-point dlci, dlci 103(0x11,0x410),
Broadcast status defined, active
Serial0/0.102 (up): point-to-point dlci, dlci 102(0x12,0x420),
broadcast status defined, active
```

1. According to the output, are DLCI 103 and DLCI 102 mapped to next-hop IP addresses?

_____

With point-to-point subinterfaces, there is no mapping between a local DLCI and a next-hop address. Each subinterface is treated as if it were a separate physical interface and each Frame Relay PVC contains only two hosts. There is no need to explicitly identify the next hop. You can also implement point-to-point subinterfaces using IP unnumbered.

Step 4

Make sure that IGRP is working by issuing the **show ip route** command as follows on SanJose1:

```
SanJose1#show ip route
Gateway of last resort is not set
C    192.168.192.0/24 is directly connected, Serial0/0.102
C    192.168.193.0/24 is directly connected, Serial0/0.102
I    192.168.194.0/24 [100/82125] via 192.168.192.2, 00:00:00, Serial0/0.102
                      [100/82125] via 192.168.193.4, 00:01:25, Serial0/0.103
I    192.168.200.0/24 [100/80135] via 192.168.192.2, 00:00:00, Serial0/0.102
I    192.168.232.0/24 [100/80135] via 192.168.193.4, 00:01:25, Serial0/0.103
C    192.168.0.0/24 is directly connected, FastEthernet0/0
```

Verify round-trip connectivity with an extended ping between the Fast Ethernet interfaces of SanJose1 and London. This ping should be successful. Troubleshoot as necessary.

Lab 6.4.4: Configuring Hub-and-Spoke Frame Relay

Estimated Time: 30 Minutes

Objective

In this lab, configure Frame Relay on three routers in a hub-and-spoke topology. Figure 6-4 shows the sample topology you use for this lab.

Figure 6-4   Sample Topology for Lab 6.4.4

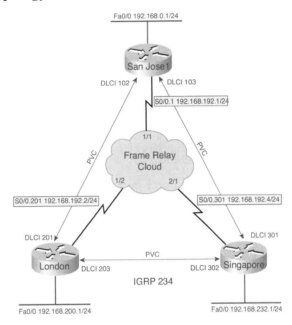

Equipment Requirements

This lab requires an Adtran Atlas 550 or similar device and 2600 or 1700 series routers.

Scenario

In an effort to cut costs, the International Travel Agency has been monitoring the internetwork traffic patterns of its full-mesh Frame Relay topology. It was determined that the PVC between London and Singapore is underutilized and that canceling the redundant PVC and implementing a hub-and-spoke topology could reduce costs. Any traffic destined for Singapore and originating in London would be relayed through SanJose1. Unfortunately, the hub in a hub-and-spoke topology creates a single point of failure. However, it is a risk that the International Travel Agency administration is willing to take.

Step 1

Before beginning this lab, reload each router after erasing its startup configuration. This step prevents problems that residual configurations might cause. After you prepare the equipment, proceed with Step 2.

Build the network according to Figure 6-4. This lab assumes that you use an Adtran Atlas 550 to emulate the Frame Relay cloud. You can use other WAN emulators or a router as a Frame Relay switch. If you use the Atlas 550, be sure to connect the serial interfaces on each router to the port on the Atlas using a V.35 cable, as labeled in the figure. Configure the appropriate host names and Fast Ethernet IP addresses on each router.

Step 2

Configure SanJose1 for IGRP (AS 234) and Frame Relay. As the hub router, SanJose1 needs to direct packets through multiple PVCs. Configuring a multipoint subinterface lets you associate one subinterface with more than one DLCI. Use the **frame-relay interface-dlci** command to specify local DLCIs, as shown in the following:

```
SanJose1(config)#interface serial 0/0
SanJose1(config-if)#encapsulation frame-relay
SanJose1(config)#interface serial 0/0.1 multipoint
SanJose1(config-subif)#ip address 192.168.192.1 255.255.255.0
SanJose1(config-subif)#frame-relay interface-dlci 103
SanJose1(config-fr-dlci)#exit
SanJose1(config-subif)#frame-relay interface-dlci 102
SanJose1(config-fr-dlci)#exit
SanJose1(config-subif)#exit
SanJose1(config)#router igrp 234
SanJose1(config-router)#network 192.168.192.0
SanJose1(config-router)#network 192.168.0.0
```

Next, configure London for IGRP (AS 234) and Frame Relay. You need only one DLCI on the spoke routers. Therefore, you can use a point-to-point subinterface. Because it is a subinterface configuration, include the **frame-relay interface-dlci** command, as shown in the following:

```
London(config)#interface serial 0/0
London(config-if)#encapsulation frame-relay
London(config)#interface serial 0/0.201 point-to-point
London(config-subif)#ip add 192.168.192.2 255.255.255.0
London(config-subif)#frame-relay interface-dlci 201
London(config-fr-dlci)#exit
London(config-subif)#exit
London(config)#router igrp 234
London(config-router)#network 192.168.200.0
London(config-router)#network 192.168.192.0
```

Use these commands as a guide and configure Singapore according to Figure 6-4.

Step 3

Test for connectivity as follows with pings between routers:

```
London#ping 192.168.192.1
Type escape sequence to abort.
Sending 5, 100-byte ICMP Echos to 192.168.192.1, timeout is 2 seconds:
!!!!!
Success rate is 100 percent (5/5), round-trip min/avg/max = 44/44/44 ms

London#ping 192.168.192.4
Type escape sequence to abort.
Sending 5, 100-byte ICMP Echos to 192.168.192.4, timeout is 2 seconds:
!!!!!
Success rate is 100 percent (5/5), round-trip min/avg/max = 88/90/92 ms
```

1.   Do the pings demonstrate successful connectivity?

In a functioning internetwork, hosts at each site must be able to communicate. You can test the complete path, from LAN to LAN, with extended pings.

First, ping from SanJose1's LAN interface (192.168.0.1) to Singapore's LAN interface (192.168.232.1). This ping should be successful. Next, ping from SanJose1's LAN interface (192.168.0.1) to London's LAN interface (192.168.200.1). This ping should also be successful.

Finally, ping from London's LAN interface to Singapore's LAN interface and back from Singapore to London. Output should be similar to the following:

```
London#ping
Protocol [ip]:
Target IP address: 192.168.232.1
Repeat count [5]:
Datagram size [100]:
Timeout in seconds [2]:
Extended commands [n]: y
Source address or interface: 192.168.200.1
Type of service [0]:
Set DF bit in IP header? [no]:
Validate reply data? [no]:
Data pattern [0xABCD]:
Loose, Strict, Record, Timestamp, Verbose[none]:
Sweep range of sizes [n]:
Type escape sequence to abort.
Sending 5, 100-byte ICMP Echos to 192.168.232.1, timeout is 2 seconds:
.....
Success rate is 0 percent (0/5)
```

These pings should fail. Because users on the London LAN cannot access the Singapore LAN, this configuration is not complete.

To isolate the problem, view the routing tables of each router. Output should be similar to the following:

```
SanJose1#show ip route

Gateway of last resort is not set
C    192.168.192.0/24 is directly connected, Serial0/0.1
I    192.168.200.0/24 [100/80135] via 192.168.192.2, 00:01:19, Serial0/0.1
I    192.168.232.0/24 [100/80135] via 192.168.192.4, 00:00:53, Serial0/0.1
C    192.168.0.0/24 is directly connected, FastEthernet0/0


London#show ip route

Gateway of last resort is not set
C    192.168.192.0/24 is directly connected, Serial0/0.201
C    192.168.200.0/24 is directly connected, FastEthernet0/0
I    192.168.0.0/24 [100/80135] via 192.168.192.1, 00:00:18, Serial0/0.201


Singapore#show ip route

Gateway of last resort is not set
C    192.168.192.0/24 is directly connected, Serial0/0.301
C    192.168.232.0/24 is directly connected, FastEthernet0/0
I    192.168.0.0/24 [100/8486] via 192.168.192.1, 00:01:06, Serial0/0.301
```

London and Singapore have not received IGRP updates about each other's LANs. However, both of these networks are properly advertised using IGRP commands, and both have been installed in SanJose1's routing table.

As the hub router, SanJose1 should forward information to the spoke routers, including routing advertisements. However, remember that distance vector routing protocols resist routing loops with the split horizon rule. This rule states that a router cannot advertise a route through the same physical interface it was received on. When you configure an interface with the **encapsulation frame-relay** command, split horizon is automatically disabled on the major interface (Serial 0/0) but is enabled by default on Frame Relay subinterfaces.

Both of the PVCs are using the same multipoint subinterface on SanJose1. Therefore, routes learned from one spoke router cannot be sent back through the same subinterface to the other spoke router. You must disable split horizon for SanJose1 to be able to send a route learned from one spoke to the other.

You can disable split horizon on SanJose1's subinterface, Serial 0/0.1, by issuing the following commands:

```
SanJose1(config)#interface serial 0/0.1 multipoint
SanJose1(config-subif)#no ip split-horizon
```

Verify this configuration by issuing the **show ip interface s0/0.1** command as follows:

```
SanJose1#show ip interface s0/0.1
Serial0/0.1 is up, line protocol is up
  Internet address is 192.168.192.1/24
  Broadcast address is 255.255.255.255
  Address determined by setup command
  MTU is 1500 bytes
  Helper address is not set
  Directed broadcast forwarding is disabled
  Outgoing access list is not set
  Inbound  access list is not set
  Proxy ARP is enabled
  Security level is default
  Split horizon is disabled
  ICMP redirects are always sent
  ICMP unreachables are always sent
  ICMP mask replies are never sent
  IP fast switching is enabled
  IP fast switching on the same interface is enabled
  IP Flow switching is disabled
  IP Feature Fast switching turbo vector
  IP multicast fast switching is enabled

  IP multicast distributed fast switching is disabled
  IP route-cache flags are Fast
  Router Discovery is disabled
```

Enter the following command to check Singapore's routing table again:

```
Singapore#show ip route
Gateway of last resort is not set
C    192.168.192.0/24 is directly connected, Serial0/0.301
I    192.168.200.0/24 [100/82135] via 192.168.192.1, 00:00:19, Serial0/0.301
C    192.168.232.0/24 is directly connected, FastEthernet0/0
I    192.168.0.0/24 [100/8486] via 192.168.192.1, 00:00:19, Serial0/0.301
```

Confirm internetwork connectivity between the Singapore and London LANs with an extended ping as follows:

```
Singapore#ping
Protocol [ip]:
Target IP address: 192.168.200.1
Repeat count [5]: 55
Datagram size [100]:
Timeout in seconds [2]:
Extended commands [n]: y
```

```
Source address or interface: 192.168.232.1
Type of service [0]:
Set DF bit in IP header? [no]:
Validate reply data? [no]:
Data pattern [0xABCD]:
Loose, Strict, Record, Timestamp, Verbose[none]:
Sweep range of sizes [n]:
Type escape sequence to abort.
Sending 55, 100-byte ICMP Echos to 192.168.200.1, timeout is 2 seconds:
!!!!!!!!!!!!!!!!!!!!!!!!!!!!!!!!!!!!!!!!!!!!!!!!!!!!!!!!!
Success rate is 100 percent (55/55), round-trip min/avg/max = 92/93/108 ms
```

If this ping is successful, all three regional sites are communicating over a hub-and-spoke Frame Relay topology.

Chapter 7

Managing Frame Relay Traffic

Lab 7.3.1: Frame Relay Subinterfaces and Traffic Shaping

Estimated Time: 50 Minutes

Objective

In this lab, you configure Frame Relay on three routers in a hub-and-spoke topology using subinterfaces and map classes. You also configure rate enforcement to control traffic rates on a per-PVC basis. Figure 7-1 shows the sample topology you use for this lab.

Figure 7-1   Sample Topology for Lab 7.3.1

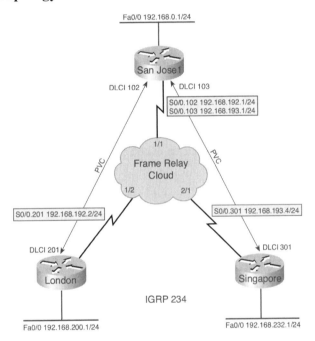

Equipment Requirements

This lab requires three routers configured as shown in Figure 7-1. You cannot use Cisco 2500 series routers in this lab because they do not have Fast Ethernet interfaces.

Scenario

Each Frame Relay link in the International Travel Agency WAN is a T1 (1.544 Mbps). After monitoring traffic patterns on the WAN, you notice that the PVC between SanJose1 and Singapore has a low average throughput. In an effort to cut costs, it is decided to revise the contract with the service provider to reduce the committed information rate (CIR) from 1.544 Mbps to 19.2 kbps.

SanJose1 transmits 80 times faster than Singapore can receive. Therefore, either the Frame Relay switches need to buffer the frames or Singapore could be flooded with traffic. Not wanting to rely on the traffic management of the Frame Relay service provider, it is decided to throttle back the rate at which SanJose1 transmits to Singapore. This choice will reduce congestion before it becomes an issue in the WAN.

Step 1

Before beginning this lab, you should reload each router after erasing its startup configuration. Taking this step prevents problems that residual configurations can cause.

Build the network according to Figure 7-1. This lab assumes that you use an Adtran Atlas 550 as the Frame Relay cloud. You can use other WAN emulators or a router as a Frame Relay switch. If you use the Atlas 550, be sure to connect the serial interfaces on the router to the port on the Atlas using a V.35 cable, as labeled in the figure.

Step 2

Configure the router with basic information such as router name and passwords as well as the LAN interfaces. In this lab, use Cisco Frame Relay encapsulation. You can explicitly configure the LMI type as ANSI or let the router autosense it. Use the basic Frame Relay information that follows to configure the routers.

Each PVC exists as a point-to-point network on its own logical IP subnet. The following is a partial configuration for SanJose1, London, and Singapore:

On SanJose1:

```
SanJose1(config)#interface serial 0/0
SanJose1(config-if)#encapsulation frame-relay
SanJose1(config-if)#no shut

SanJose1(config)#interface serial 0/0.103 point-to-point
SanJose1(config-subif)#ip address 192.168.193.1 255.255.255.0
SanJose1(config-subif)#frame-relay interface-dlci 103
SanJose1(config-fr-dlci)#exit

SanJose1(config-subif)#interface serial 0/0.102 point-to-point
SanJose1(config-subif)#ip address 192.168.192.1 255.255.255.0
SanJose1(config-subif)#frame-relay interface-dlci 102

SanJose1(config)#router igrp 234
SanJose1(config-router)#network 192.168.0.0
SanJose1(config-router)#network 192.168.192.0
SanJose1(config-router)#network 192.168.193.0
```

On London:

```
London(config)#interface serial 0/0
London(config-if)#encapsulation frame-relay
London(config-if)#no shut

London(config)#interface serial 0/0.201 point-to-point
London(config-subif)#ip address 192.168.192.2 255.255.255.0
London(config-subif)#frame-relay interface-dlci 201
London(config-fr-dlci)#exit

London(config)#router igrp 234
London(config-router)#network 192.168.200.0
London(config-router)#network 192.168.192.0
```

On Singapore:

```
Singapore(config)#interface serial 0/0
Singapore(config-if)#encapsulation frame-relay
Singapore(config-if)#no shut

Singapore(config)#interface serial 0/0.301 point-to-point
Singapore(config-subif)#ip address 192.168.193.4 255.255.255.0
Singapore(config-subif)#frame-relay interface-dlci 301
Singapore(config-fr-dlci)#exit

Singapore(config)#router igrp 234
Singapore(config-router)#network 192.168.232.0
Singapore(config-router)#network 192.168.193.0
```

Step 3

Test connectivity with extended pings between the LANs of the different regional sites. From SanJose1, use an extended ping to test connectivity with London. To measure throughput, send several large packets with datagram sizes over 1000 bytes each:

```
SanJose1#ping
Protocol [ip]:
Target IP address: 192.168.200.1
Repeat count [5]: 55
Datagram size [100]: 1111
Timeout in seconds [2]:
Extended commands [n]: y
Source address or interface: 192.168.0.1
Type of service [0]:
Set DF bit in IP header? [no]:
Validate reply data? [no]:
Data pattern [0xABCD]:
Loose, Strict, Record, Timestamp, Verbose[none]:
Sweep range of sizes [n]:
Type escape sequence to abort.
Sending 55, 1111-byte ICMP Echoes to 192.168.200.1, timeout is 2
seconds:
!!!!!!!!!!!!!!!!!!!!!!!!!!!!!!!!!!!!!!!!!!!!!!!!!!!!!!!!!!!
Success rate is 100 percent (55/55), round-trip min/avg/max = 176/179/192 ms
```

1. Note the round-trip times in milliseconds.

_____

2. Using the same parameters, ping from SanJose1 to Singapore. Note the round-trip times in milliseconds.

_____

3. Finally, repeat the process and ping from London to Singapore. Note the round-trip times in milliseconds.

_____

Round-trip times vary, primarily due to the WAN interface card in the router. The router probably contains either a WIC-2A/S supporting up to 128 kbps or a WIC-2T supporting up to 2.048 Mbps. For the purposes of this lab, either WIC is fine. The round-trip times will become relevant when you compare them to the results of later tests.

Step 4

You must change the CIR between SanJose1 and Singapore from 1.544 Mbps to 19.2 kbps. Create a map class in global configuration mode defining the CIR on both Singapore and SanJose1. You must assign a logical name to uniquely identify each map class. Use **CIR** as the map class name:

```
Singapore(config)#map-class frame-relay CIR
Singapore(config-map-class)#frame-relay traffic-rate 19200

SanJose1(config)#map-class frame-relay CIR
SanJose1(config-map-class)#frame-relay traffic-rate 19200
```

Any Frame Relay interface can use a Frame Relay map class. In this case, you apply the map class to Singapore's subinterface, as shown in the following configuration. Because the map class specifies rate enforcement, you must enable Frame Relay traffic shaping on the major interface:

```
Singapore(config)#interface serial 0/0
Singapore(config-if)#frame-relay traffic-shaping
Singapore(config-if)#interface serial 0/0.301 point-to-point
Singapore(config-subif)#frame-relay class CIR
```

Configure the other end of this PVC, on SanJose1, using the same commands as follows:

```
SanJose1(config)#interface serial 0/0
SanJose1(config-if)#frame-relay traffic-shaping
SanJose1(config-if)#interface serial 0/0.103 point-to-point
SanJose1(config-subif)#frame-relay class CIR
```

Step 5

Test connectivity and throughput with extended pings as before, recording round-trip times. The average and round-trip times should have increased as traffic was buffered due to slow WAN links. The following are some sample results:

```
SanJose1#ping
*******output omitted********
Sending 55, 1111-byte ICMP Echoes to 192.168.232.1, timeout is 2 seconds:
!!!!!!!!!!!!!!!!!!!!!!!!!!!!!!!!!!!!!!!!!!!!!!!!!!!!!!!!!!!
Success rate is 100 percent (55/55),round-trip min/avg/max = 184/460/520 ms

London#ping
*******output omitted********
Sending 55, 1111-byte ICMP Echoes to 192.168.232.1, timeout is 2 seconds:
!!!!!!!!!!!!!!!!!!!!!!!!!!!!!!!!!!!!!!!!!!!!!!!!!!!!!!!!!!!
Success rate is 100 percent (55/55),round-trip min/avg/max = 356/464/540 ms
```

1. How are the **ping** command results different from the first set of pings that you ran in Step 3?

_____

_____

Step 6

To observe detailed traffic shaping statistics, issue **show frame-relay pvc 103** on SanJose1. Although traffic shaping is enabled, it is only active if traffic is buffered. For this reason, "shaping inactive" might appear in the output of this command, as in the following sample output:

```
SanJose1#show frame-relay pvc 103

PVC Statistics for interface Serial0/0 (Frame Relay DTE)

DLCI = 103, DLCI USAGE = LOCAL, PVC STATUS = ACTIVE, INTERFACE =
Serial0/0.103
  input pkts 82           output pkts 80          in bytes 14127
  out bytes 13930         dropped pkts 1          in FECN pkts 0
  in BECN pkts 0          out FECN pkts 0         out BECN pkts 0
  in DE pkts 0            out DE pkts 0
  out bcast pkts 66          out bcast bytes 12983
  pvc create time 00:39:54, last time pvc status changed 00:03:00
  cir 19200        bc 19200      be 0        limit 300      interval 125
  mincir 9600      byte increment 300    BECN response no
  pkts 17        bytes 2828      pkts delayed 0          bytes delayed 0
  shaping inactive
  traffic shaping drops 0
  Serial0/0.102 dlci 102 is first come first serve default queuing
  Output queue 0/40, 0 drop, 0 dequeued
```

1.   According to the output of the **show frame-relay pvc 103** command, what is the CIR of this PVC?

Lab 7.3.2: Frame Relay Traffic Shaping with Class-Based Weighted Fair Queuing

Estimated Time: 50 Minutes

Objective

In this lab, you configure Enhanced Interior Gateway Routing Protocol (EIGRP) and Frame Relay on three routers in a hub-and-spoke topology using subinterfaces. You also configure class-based weighted fair queuing (CBWFQ) with Frame Relay traffic shaping. Figure 7-2 shows the sample topology for this lab.

Figure 7-2   Sample Topology for Lab 7.3.2

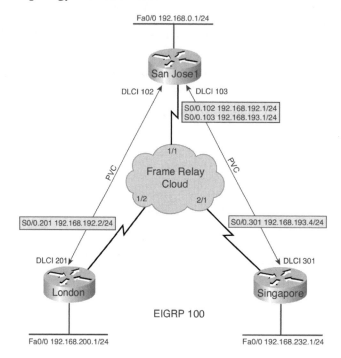

Equipment Requirements

This lab requires three routers configured as shown in Figure 7-2. You cannot use Cisco 2500 series routers in this lab because they do not have Fast Ethernet interfaces.

Scenario

SanJose1 transmits data 80 times faster than Singapore or London can receive. The Frame Relay switches need to buffer the excess frames or Singapore and London could be flooded with traffic. It is not advisable to rely on the traffic management of the Frame Relay service provider. Therefore, it is decided to use CBWFQ with Frame Relay traffic shaping to throttle back the rate at which SanJose1 transmits to Singapore and London. This choice will reduce congestion before it becomes an issue in the Frame Relay WAN.

Step 1

Before beginning this lab, reload each router after erasing its startup configuration. This step prevents problems that residual configurations might cause.

Build the network according to Figure 7-2. This lab assumes that you use an Adtran Atlas 550 as the Frame Relay cloud. You can use other WAN emulators or a router as a Frame Relay switch. If you use the Atlas 550, be sure to connect the serial interfaces on the routers to the port on the Atlas using a V.35 cable, as labeled in the figure.

Step 2

Configure the router with basic information such as router name and passwords as well as the LAN interfaces. In this lab, use Cisco Frame Relay encapsulation. Use the basic Frame Relay information that follows to configure all three routers.

On SanJose1:

```
SanJose1(config)#interface serial 0/0
SanJose1(config-if)#encapsulation frame-relay
SanJose1(config-if)#no shut

SanJose1(config-subif)#interface serial 0/0.102 point-to-point
SanJose1(config-subif)#ip address 192.168.192.1 255.255.255.0
SanJose1(config-subif)#frame-relay interface-dlci 102
SanJose1(config-fr-dlci)#exit

SanJose1(config)#interface serial 0/0.103 point-to-point
SanJose1(config-subif)#ip address 192.168.193.1 255.255.255.0
SanJose1(config-subif)#frame-relay interface-dlci 103
```

On London:

```
London(config)#interface serial 0/0
London(config-if)#encapsulation frame-relay
London(config-if)#no shut

London(config)#interface serial 0/0.201 point-to-point
London(config-subif)#ip address 192.168.192.2 255.255.255.0
London(config-subif)#frame-relay interface-dlci 201
London(config-fr-dlci)#exit
```

On Singapore:

```
Singapore(config)#interface serial 0/0
Singapore(config-if)#encapsulation frame-relay
Singapore(config-if)#no shut

Singapore(config)#interface serial 0/0.301 point-to-point
Singapore(config-subif)#ip address 192.168.193.4 255.255.255.0
Singapore(config-subif)#frame-relay interface-dlci 301
Singapore(config-fr-dlci)#exit
```

Step 3

Configure EIGRP on all routers as indicated for AS 100. The following configuration displays the EIGRP configurations for SanJose1:

```
SanJose1(config)#router eigrp 100
SanJose1(config-router)#network 192.168.0.0
SanJose1(config-router)#network 192.168.192.0
SanJose1(config-router)#network 192.168.193.0
```

Use **ping** and **show ip route** to verify the work and to test connectivity between all routers.

Step 4

Define a class map that will establish the match criteria for identifying data belonging in a policy class. Place all traffic from the SanJose1 192.168.0.0 network that is destined for the Singapore and the London LAN into a policy class. Enter the following to create an extended access list that will identify data that belongs in a class:

```
SanJose1(config)#access-list 101 permit ip 192.168.0.0 0.0.0.255 192.168.200.0
    0.0.0.255
SanJose1(config)#access-list 101 permit ip 192.168.0.0 0.0.0.255 192.168.232.0
    0.0.0.255

SanJose1(config)#class-map CBWFQ
SanJose1(config-cmap)#match access-group 101
```

The **class-map** command creates a class called CBWFQ. You use the **match** command to identify access list 101 as packets that belong in a class.

Step 5

Configure a class policy by specifying CBWFQ-TS as the name of the policy map. You define the class policy by specifying the bandwidth guarantee for the CBWFQ traffic class:

```
SanJose1(config)#policy-map CBWFQ-TS
SanJose1(config-pmap)#class CBWFQ
SanJose1(config-pmap-c)#bandwidth 50
```

The **bandwidth** command specifies the bandwidth for traffic in the CBWFQ class. CBWFQ derives the weight for packets belonging to the class from the bandwidth allocated to the class. CBFWQ then uses the weight to ensure that the queue for the class is serviced fairly.

To attach the policy map to a Frame Relay serial interface, you must apply the **service-policy** command to a Frame Relay map class.

Step 6

On SanJose1, create a map class in global configuration mode defining Frame Relay traffic shaping parameters. You must assign a logical name to uniquely identify each map class. Use FRTS as the name. The following configuration displays the traffic shaping parameters for SanJose1:

```
SanJose1(config)#map-class frame-relay FRTS
SanJose1(config-map-class)#frame-relay adaptive-shaping becn
SanJose1(config-map-class)#frame-relay cir 64000
SanJose1(config-map-class)#frame-relay bc 8000
SanJose1(config-map-class)#frame-relay mincir 56000
SanJose1(config-map-class)#service-policy output CBWFQ-TS
```

The **frame-relay adaptive-shaping becn** command uses Backward Explicit Congestion Notification (BECN) notices from the Frame Relay switch as the congestion backward notification mechanism. From these notices, traffic shaping will adapt. The optional **frame-relay cir** command sets the CIR to 64 kbps. The **frame-relay bc optional** command sets the committed burst rate to 8000 bps. The **frame-relay mincir** command sets the minimum acceptable CIR to 56 kbps. The **service-policy output** command attaches the CBWFQ-TS policy class to the Frame Relay map class.

Step 7

Any Frame Relay interface can use a Frame Relay map class. In this case, you apply the map class FRTS to both of the SanJose1 subinterfaces, as follows:

```
SanJose1(config)#interface serial 0/0
SanJose1(config-if)#frame-relay traffic-shaping
SanJose1(config-if)#interface serial 0/0.102
SanJose1(config-subif)#frame-relay class FRTS
SanJose1(config-if)#interface serial 0/0.103
SanJose1(config-subif)#frame-relay class FRTS
```

Note: Because the map class specifies traffic shaping parameters, you must enable Frame Relay traffic shaping on the major interface.

Step 8

To observe detailed traffic shaping statistics, issue **show frame-relay pvc 103** on SanJose1:

```
SanJose1#show frame pvc 103

PVC Statistics for interface Serial0/0 (Frame Relay DTE)

DLCI = 103, DLCI USAGE = LOCAL, PVC STATUS = ACTIVE, INTERFACE =
  Serial0/0.103

  input pkts 52          output pkts 6           in bytes 4732
  out bytes 1836         dropped pkts 0          in pkts dropped 0
  out pkts dropped 0           out bytes dropped 0
  in FECN pkts 0         in BECN pkts 0          out FECN pkts 0
  out BECN pkts 0        in DE pkts 0            out DE pkts 0
  out bcast pkts 6       out bcast bytes 1836
  Shaping adapts to BECN
  pvc create time 00:06:00, last time pvc status changed 00:03:38
  cir 64000      bc 8000      be 0        byte limit 1000    interval 125
  mincir 56000      byte increment 1000  Adaptive Shaping BECN
  pkts 6          bytes 1836      pkts delayed 0        bytes delayed 0
  shaping inactive
  traffic shaping drops 0
  service policy CBWFQ-TS
 Serial0/0.103: DLCI 103 -

  Service-policy output: CBWFQ-TS

    Class-map: CBWFQ (match-all)
      0 packets, 0 bytes
      5 minute offered rate 0 bps, drop rate 0 bps
      Match: access-group 101
      Queueing
        Output Queue: Conversation 25
        Bandwidth 50 (kbps) Max Threshold 64 (packets)
        (pkts matched/bytes matched) 0/0
        (depth/total drops/no-buffer drops) 0/0/0

    Class-map: class-default (match-any)
      6 packets, 1836 bytes
      5 minute offered rate 0 bps, drop rate 0 bps
      Match: any
  Output queue size 0/max total 600/drops 0
```

1.   According to the **show frame pvc 103** command output, what is the CIR of this PVC 103?

Step 9

To display the configuration of the service policy map, use the **show policy-map** command. It displays all class configurations of any existing service policy maps, shown as follows:

```
SanJose1#show policy-map
  Policy Map CBWFQ-TS
    Class CBWFQ
      Bandwidth 50 (kbps) Max Threshold 64 (packets)
```

You can also display the configuration of all policy classes on an interface configured for a service policy. The following output shows the configurations for the CBWFQ-TS class:

```
SanJose1#show policy-map interface
 Serial0/0.102: DLCI 102 -

  Service-policy output: CBWFQ-TS

    Class-map: CBWFQ (match-all)
      0 packets, 0 bytes
      5 minute offered rate 0 bps, drop rate 0 bps
      Match: access-group 101
      Queueing
        Output Queue: Conversation 25
        Bandwidth 50 (kbps) Max Threshold 64 (packets)
        (pkts matched/bytes matched) 0/0
        (depth/total drops/no-buffer drops) 0/0/0

    Class-map: class-default (match-any)
      9 packets, 2718 bytes
      5 minute offered rate 0 bps, drop rate 0 bps
      Match: any
 Serial0/0.103: DLCI 103 -

  Service-policy output: CBWFQ-TS

    Class-map: CBWFQ (match-all)
      0 packets, 0 bytes
      5 minute offered rate 0 bps, drop rate 0 bps
      Match: access-group 101
      Queueing
        Output Queue: Conversation 25
        Bandwidth 50 (kbps) Max Threshold 64 (packets)
        (pkts matched/bytes matched) 0/0
        (depth/total drops/no-buffer drops) 0/0/0

    Class-map: class-default (match-any)
      8 packets, 2448 bytes
      5 minute offered rate 0 bps, drop rate 0 bps
      Match: any
```

Chapter 8

WAN Backup

Lab 8.7.1: Configuring ISDN Dial Backup

Estimated Time: 45 Minutes

Objective

In this lab, you configure ISDN dial backup for a fixed Frame Relay WAN link. Figure 8-1 shows the sample topology for this lab.

Figure 8-1   Sample Topology for Lab 8.7.1

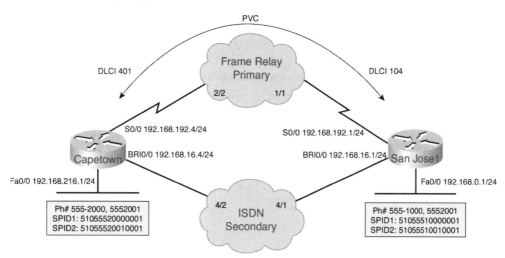

Equipment Requirements

This lab requires two routers and an Adtran or similar device, configured as shown in Figure 8-1.

Scenario

The network engineer for the International Travel Agency is responsible for full-time WAN connectivity between regional headquarters and San Jose company headquarters. Frame Relay permanent virtual circuits (PVC) have been made into a star topology, with SanJose1 as the hub router. To provide fault tolerance, each Frame Relay PVC is backed up with ISDN Basic Rate Interface (BRI).

Step 1

Build the network as shown in Figure 8-1. If you use the Atlas 550 as a WAN emulator, be sure to use the ports as indicated in the figure. Before beginning this lab, you should reload each router after erasing its startup configuration. Taking this step prevents problems that residual configurations might cause.

Step 2

Use the following to configure and test ISDN BRI on Capetown, using Challenge Handshake Authentication Protocol (CHAP) authentication:

```
Capetown(config)#isdn switch-type basic-ni
Capetown(config)#username SanJose1 password cisco
Capetown(config)#dialer-list 1 protocol ip permit
Capetown(config)#interface bri 0/0
Capetown(config-if)#ip address 192.168.16.4 255.255.255.0
Capetown(config-if)#encapsulation ppp
Capetown(config-if)#ppp authentication chap
Capetown(config-if)#isdn spid1 51055520000001 5552000
Capetown(config-if)#isdn spid2 51055520010001 5552001
Capetown(config-if)#dialer map ip 192.168.16.1 name SanJose1 broadcast 5551000
Capetown(config-if)#dialer idle-timeout 60
Capetown(config-if)#dialer-group 1
Capetown(config-if)#no shutdown
```

Next, configure SanJose1 as shown in the following:

```
SanJose1(config)#isdn switch-type basic-ni
SanJose1(config)#username Capetown password cisco
SanJose1(config)#dialer-list 1 protocol ip permit
SanJose1(config)#interface bri 0/0
SanJose1(config-if)#ip address 192.168.16.1 255.255.255.0
SanJose1(config-if)#encapsulation ppp
SanJose1(config-if)#ppp authentication chap
SanJose1(config-if)#isdn spid1 51055510000001 5551000
SanJose1(config-if)#isdn spid2 51055510010001 5551001
SanJose1(config-if)#dialer map ip 192.168.16.4 name Capetown broadcast
SanJose1(config-if)#dialer idle-timeout 60
SanJose1(config-if)#dialer-group 1
SanJose1(config-if)#no shutdown
```

Note: SanJose1 only accepts BRI calls, so do not configure a phone number with the **dialer map** statement.

Ping across the ISDN link from Capetown to SanJose1 (192.168.16.1). This ping should be successful. Troubleshoot as necessary.

Step 3

Configure and test Frame Relay connectivity on both routers. The following is an example of the Capetown configuration:

```
Capetown(config)#interface s0/0
Capetown(config-if)#ip address 192.168.192.4 255.255.255.0
Capetown(config-if)#encapsulation frame-relay
Capetown(config-if)#frame-relay map ip 192.168.192.1 401 broadcast
Capetown(config-if)#no shutdown
```

Use **ping** to verify that the Frame Relay link is operational. Ping one serial interface from the other.

Step 4

Configure and test static routing between the Capetown spoke router and the SanJose1 hub router. Because Capetown supports a stub network, create a static route to all unknown networks pointing at SanJose1. SanJose1 uses a specific static route to return packets to the Capetown LAN, as shown in the following:

```
SanJose1(config)#ip route 192.168.216.0 255.255.255.0 192.168.192.4
Capetown(config)#ip route 0.0.0.0 0.0.0.0 192.168.192.1
```

Verify that the static routing configuration works by performing extended pings between LANs.

Step 5

Configure ISDN dialup backup routing.

The Frame Relay link has adequate bandwidth for normal traffic. The ISDN BRI is deployed only for fault tolerance. The service provider charges for each minute of ISDN call time if the defined data transfer levels are exceeded. Having a redundant path is worth the cost, but you should minimize use of the line to avoid associated charges.

Use the following configuration to place floating static routes between SanJose1 and Capetown, utilizing the ISDN link:

```
Capetown(config)#ip route 0.0.0.0 0.0.0.0 192.168.16.1 222
SanJose1(config)#ip route 192.168.216.0 255.255.255.0 192.168.16.4 222
```

The following are views of the routing tables:

```
SanJose1#show ip route
Gateway of last resort is not set
C    192.168.192.0/24 is directly connected, Serial0/0
S    192.168.216.0/24 [1/0] via 192.168.192.4
C    192.168.16.0/24 is directly connected, BRI0/0
C    192.168.0.0/24 is directly connected, FastEthernet0/0

Capetown#show ip route
Gateway of last resort is 192.168.192.1 to network 0.0.0.0
C    192.168.192.0/24 is directly connected, Serial0/0
C    192.168.216.0/24 is directly connected, FastEthernet0/0
C    192.168.16.0/24 is directly connected, BRI0/0
S*   0.0.0.0/0 [1/0] via 192.168.192.1
```

1.   Although you configure two static routes on each router, only one of those routes is installed in each routing table. Why?

_____

_____

The static routes using the Frame Relay link have a default administrative distance of 1. These routes are preferred over all routes except directly connected routes, which have an administrative distance of 0. If the Frame Relay link fails, associated routes are eventually removed from the routing table. ISDN routes with an administrative distance of 222 are then placed in the routing table. Connectivity is restored, although at a much slower rate.

The ISDN link is to be active only in the event of a Frame Relay link failure. Enter the following configuration to make BRI 0/0 a backup interface to Serial0/0 on Capetown:

```
Capetown(config)#interface s0/0
Capetown(config-if)#backup interface bri0/0
Capetown(config-if)#backup delay 6 8
```

You configure only Capetown with the **backup interface** and **backup delay** commands. The first backup delay value, 6, represents the number of seconds between Serial 0/0 failure and the backup link (BRI 0/0) becoming active. The second value, 8, is the number of seconds after Serial 0/0 is restored before bringing down the backup link. If you configured the SanJose1 BRI as a backup interface, Capetown could not establish a dialup connection with SanJose1. The SanJose1 BRI would either be in standby mode or trying to make a dialup call. In either case, Capetown would not be able to connect with it.

The following is another look at the Capetown routing table:

```
Capetown#show ip route
Gateway of last resort is 192.168.192.1 to network 0.0.0.0
C    192.168.192.0/24 is directly connected, Serial0/0
C    192.168.216.0/24 is directly connected, FastEthernet0/0
S*   0.0.0.0/0 [1/0] via 192.168.192.1
```

The directly connected route for the ISDN link has disappeared. Enter the following to check whether the BRI is down by issuing the **show interface** command on Capetown:

```
Capetown#show interface bri0/0
BRI0/0 is standby mode, line protocol is down
  Hardware is PQUICC BRI with U interface
  Internet address is 192.168.16.4/24
  MTU 1500 bytes, BW 64 Kbit, DLY 20000 usec,
     reliability 255/255, txload 1/255, rxload 1/255
  Encapsulation PPP, loopback not set
********output omitted********
```

The output of this command shows that the line is down but standing by, in the event the serial interface goes down.

On Capetown, issue the **show backup** command as shown in the following:

```
Capetown#show backup
Primary Interface   Secondary Interface   Status
----------------    -------------------   ------
Serial0/0           BRI0/0                normal operation
```

Step 6

Enter the following to test dial backup with an extended ping between Capetown and SanJose1:

```
Capetown#ping
Protocol [ip]:
Target IP address: 192.168.0.1
Repeat count [5]: 555
Datagram size [100]:
Timeout in seconds [2]: 1
Extended commands [n]: y
Source address or interface: 192.168.216.1
Type of service [0]:
Set DF bit in IP header? [no]:
Validate reply data? [no]:
Data pattern [0xABCD]:
Loose, Strict, Record, Timestamp, Verbose[none]:
Sweep range of sizes [n]:
Type escape sequence to abort.
Sending 555, 100-byte ICMP Echos to 192.168.0.1, timeout is 1
seconds:
!!!!!!!!!!!!!!!!!!!!!!!!!!!!!!!!!!!!!!!!!!!!!!!!!!!!!!!!!!!!!!!!!!!!!!
!!!!!!!!!!!!!!!!!!!!!!!!!!!!!!!!!!!!!!!!!!!!!!!!!!!!!!!!!!!!!!!!!!!!!!
!!!!........!!!!!!!!!!!!!!!!!!!!!!!!!!!!!!!!!!!!!!!!!!!!!!!!!!!!!!!!!!
!!!!!!!!!!!!!!!!!!!!!!!!!!!!!!!!!!!!!!!!!!!!!!!!!!!!!!!!!!!!!!!!!!!!!!
!!!!!!!!!!!!!!!!!!!!!!!!!!!!!!!!!!!!!!!!!!!!!!!!!!!!!!!!!!!!!!!!!!!!!!
```

```
!!!!!!!!!!!!!!!!!!!!!!!!!!!!!!!!!!!!!!!!!!!!!!!!!!!!!!!!!!!!!!!!!!!!!!!!!!!!!!!!
!!!!!!!!!!!!!!!!!!!!!!!!!!!!!!!!!!!!!!!!!!!!!!!!!!!!!!!!!!!!!!!!!!!!!!!!!!!!!!!!
!!!!!!!!!!!!!!!!!!!!!!!!!!!!!!!!!!!!!!!!!!!!!!!!!!!!!!!!!!!!!!!!!!!!!!!!!!!!!!
Success rate is 98 percent (545/555), round-trip min/avg/max = 32/39/60 ms
```

Note: While the ping progresses, disconnect the serial cable from both routers.

It took more than 5 seconds for ISDN to become active after Frame Relay failed. While active, the backup interface is in backup mode. Issue the **show backup** command on Capetown, as shown in the following:

```
Capetown#show backup
Primary Interface      Secondary Interface    Status
----------------       -------------------    ------
Serial0/0              BRI0/0                 backup mode
```

1.   How did Capetown get to SanJose1 if the only route was through the failed Frame Relay link?

_____

To verify the answer to Question 1, issue **show ip route** on Capetown. The following route should now be in the Capetown routing table:

```
C   192.168.16.0/24 is directly connected, BRI0/0
```

When Serial 0/0 failed, its associated static route was removed from the routing table and replaced by the floating static route over the ISDN link.

Enter the following to verify that the SanJose1 ISDN interface is up by issuing the **show interface bri0/0** command:

```
SanJose1#show interface bri0/0
BRI0/0 is up, line protocol is up (spoofing)
  Hardware is PQUICC BRI with U interface
  Internet address is 192.168.16.1/24
  MTU 1500 bytes, BW 64 Kbit, DLY 20000 usec,
     reliability 255/255, txload 1/255, rxload 1/255
  Encapsulation PPP, loopback not set
********output omitted********
```

The dial backup for WAN connectivity is now successfully implemented.

Save your configuration file for use with the next lab.

Lab 8.7.2: Using Secondary Links for On-Demand Bandwidth

Estimated Time: 30 Minutes

Objective

In this lab, you configure ISDN dial-on-demand bandwidth supporting overload traffic from the primary Frame Relay link. Figure 8-2 shows the sample topology you use for this lab.

Figure 8-2   Sample Topology for Lab 8.7.2

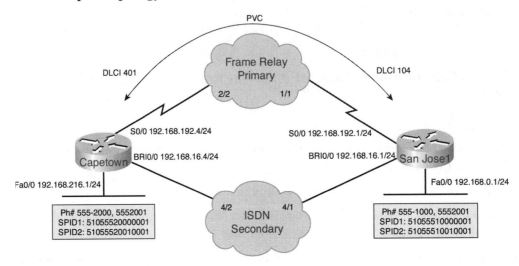

Equipment Requirements

This lab requires two routers, two hosts, and an Adtran or similar device, configured as shown in Figure 8-2.

Scenario

The International Travel Agency has expanded, increasing traffic between Capetown and SanJose1. It is waiting for the service provider to provision greater bandwidth on the Frame Relay link. In the meantime, configure ISDN to carry traffic in case the Frame Relay link becomes saturated.

Step 1

Build the network as shown in Figure 8-2. If you use the Atlas 550 as a WAN emulator, be sure to use the ports as indicated in the figure. Before beginning this lab, reload each router after erasing its startup configuration. This step prevents problems that residual configurations can cause.

Step 2

Use the following to configure and test ISDN BRI on Capetown, using CHAP authentication:

```
Capetown(config)#isdn switch-type basic-ni
Capetown(config)#username SanJose1 password cisco
Capetown(config)#dialer-list 1 protocol ip permit
Capetown(config)#interface bri 0/0
Capetown(config-if)#ip address 192.168.16.4 255.255.255.0
Capetown(config-if)#encapsulation ppp
Capetown(config-if)#ppp authentication chap
```

```
Capetown(config-if)#isdn spid1 51055520000001 5552000
Capetown(config-if)#isdn spid2 51055520010001 5552001
Capetown(config-if)#dialer map ip 192.168.16.1 name SanJose1 broadcast
  5551000
Capetown(config-if)#dialer idle-timeout 60
Capetown(config-if)#dialer-group 1
```

Next, configure SanJose1 as shown in the following:

```
SanJose1(config)#isdn switch-type basic-ni
SanJose1(config)#username Capetown password cisco
SanJose1(config)#dialer-list 1 protocol ip permit
SanJose1(config)#interface bri 0/0
SanJose1(config-if)#ip address 192.168.16.1 255.255.255.0
SanJose1(config-if)#encapsulation ppp
SanJose1(config-if)#ppp authentication chap
SanJose1(config-if)#isdn spid1 51055510000001 5551000
SanJose1(config-if)#isdn spid2 51055510010001 5551001
SanJose1(config-if)#dialer map ip 192.168.16.4 name Capetown broadcast
SanJose1(config-if)#dialer idle-timeout 60
SanJose1(config-if)#dialer-group 1
```

Note: SanJose1 only accepts BRI calls, so do not configure a phone number with the **dialer map** statement.

Ping across the ISDN link from Capetown to SanJose1 (192.168.16.1). This ping should be successful. Troubleshoot as necessary.

ISDN is to become active as the Frame Relay link reaches a predefined traffic threshold. Configure Capetown with the following syntax:

```
Capetown(config)#interface serial 0/0
Capetown(config-if)#backup load 2 1
```

The first number in the **backup load** command is the percentage of bandwidth utilization necessary on Serial 0/0 to trigger the activation of backup interface BRI 0/0. The second number is the percentage of bandwidth utilization on Serial 0/0 required to deactivate BRI 0/0. Because of the sporadic nature of data communications, percentages are evaluated, by default, during a sliding 5-second window.

Note: The **backup load** values configured in this lab are low to demonstrate functionality. In a production network, you would define load values to avoid saturation of the Frame Relay link. An example is **backup load 60 20**.

Confirm backup configuration by using the following command:

```
Capetown#show interface serial 0/0
Serial0/0 is up, line protocol is up
  Hardware is PowerQUICC Serial
  Internet address is 192.168.192.4/24
  Backup interface BRI0/0, failure delay 0 sec, secondary disable
delay 0 sec,
  kickin load 2%, kickout load 1%
  MTU 1500 bytes, BW 128 Kbit, DLY 20000 usec,
     reliability 255/255, txload 1/255, rxload 1/255
  Encapsulation FRAME-RELAY, loopback not set
```

Step 3

Both routes need to be available during times of excessive traffic, so you use equal administrative distances. Configure static routes associated with BRI 0/0 interfaces on both routers, as shown in the following:

```
Capetown(config)#ip route 0.0.0.0 0.0.0.0 192.168.192.1
Capetown(config)#ip route 0.0.0.0 0.0.0.0 192.168.16.1

SanJose1(config)#ip route 192.168.216.0 255.255.255.0 192.168.192.4
SanJose1(config)#ip route 192.168.216.0 255.255.255.0 192.168.16.4
```

As the backup interface is activated, both routes can coexist in the routing table. This arrangement allows load balancing between the two equal cost paths.

Step 4

Test the dial-on-demand bandwidth by loading the Frame Relay link over 2 percent with an extended ping from Capetown to SanJose1. Watch the BRI router interface while pinging. One channel light activates when ISDN is triggered. As soon as the ping is complete, issue the **show backup** and **show ip route** commands, as follows:

```
Capetown#ping
Protocol [ip]:
Target IP address: 192.168.0.1
Repeat count [5]: 55
Datagram size [100]: 1500
Timeout in seconds [2]: 1
Extended commands [n]: y
Source address or interface: 192.168.216.1
Type of service [0]:
Set DF bit in IP header? [no]:
Validate reply data? [no]:
Data pattern [0xABCD]:
Loose, Strict, Record, Timestamp, Verbose[none]:
Sweep range of sizes [n]:
Type escape sequence to abort.
Sending 55, 1500-byte ICMP Echos to 192.168.0.1, timeout is 1
seconds:
!!!!!!!!!!!!!!!!!!!!!!!!!!!!!!..!!!!!!!!!!!!!!!!!!!!!!!!!!!!
Success rate is 96 percent (53/55), round-trip min/avg/max = 380/418/444 ms

Capetown#show backup
Primary Interface      Secondary Interface      Status
----------------       -------------------      ------
Serial0/0              BRI0/0                   overload mode


Capetown#show ip route
Gateway of last resort is 192.168.192.1 to network 0.0.0.0
C    192.168.192.0/24 is directly connected, Serial0/0
C    192.168.216.0/24 is directly connected, FastEthernet0/0
     192.168.16.0/24 is variably subnetted, 2 subnets, 2 masks
C        192.168.16.0/24 is directly connected, BRI0/0
C        192.168.16.1/32 is directly connected, BRI0/0
S*   0.0.0.0/0 [1/0] via 192.168.192.1
                [1/0] via 192.168.16.1
```

There are two parallel routes to SanJose1 while the BRI 0/0 interface is up. ISDN activated at about the same time the two packets were dropped due to congestion.

As follows, issue **show backup** after 1 minute or after the BRI 0/0 channel light turns off:

```
Capetown#show backup
Primary Interface    Secondary Interface    Status
-----------------    -------------------    ------
Serial0/0            BRI0/0                 normal operation
```

The BRI 0/0 interface has deactivated and returned to standby mode. The **show ip interface brief** command, as the following shows, is another command that you can use to check interface status:

```
Capetown#show ip interface brief
Interface            IP-Address       OK? Method Status          Protocol
FastEthernet0/0      192.168.216.1    YES NVRAM  up              up
Serial0/0            192.168.192.4    YES NVRAM  up              up
BRI0/0               192.168.16.4     YES NVRAM  standby mode    down
BRI0/0:1             unassigned       YES unset  administratively down down
BRI0/0:2             unassigned       YES unset  administratively down down
Serial0/1            unassigned       YES NVRAM  administratively down down
```

Dial-on-demand bandwidth is now successfully configured.

Lab 8.7.3: Configuring Dialer Backup with Dialer Profiles

Estimated Time: 45 Minutes

Objective

In this lab, you configure ISDN dial backup with dialer profiles. Figure 8-3 shows the topology in this lab.

Figure 8-3   Sample Topology for Lab 8.7.3

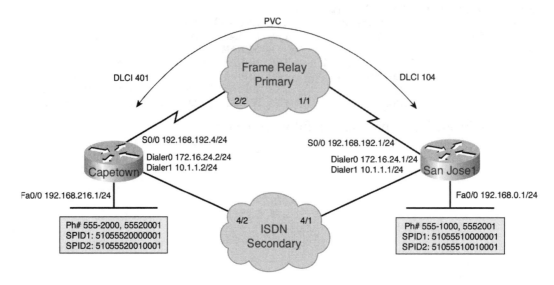

Equipment Requirements

This lab requires two routers, two hosts, and an Adtran or similar device, configured as shown in Figure 8-3.

Scenario

To ensure full time point-to-point WAN connectivity between SanJose1 and Capetown, you previously configured ISDN dial backup using the physical BRI interface, with the techniques discussed in Lab 8.7.1, "Configuring ISDN Dial Backup." If you configure the physical BRI interface for dial backup, you can enable either dial backup or traffic overload but not both. To overcome this limitation, configure dial backup using dialer profiles. If you use dialer profiles for dial backup, you can use an idle ISDN connection for load balancing and dial backup.

Step 1

Build the network as shown in Figure 8-3. If you use the Atlas 550 as a WAN emulator, be sure to use the ports as indicated in the figure. Before beginning this lab, reload each router after erasing its startup configuration. This step prevents problems that residual configurations can cause.

Step 2

Configure SanJose1 and Capetown to use the appropriate ISDN switch type, National ISDN-1. You use PPP encapsulation and CHAP on the B channels. Therefore, enter the case-sensitive username and password information on both routers, as shown in the following:

```
SanJose1(config)#isdn switch-type basic-ni
SanJose1(config)#username Capetown password cisco
SanJose1(config)#username jill password cisco
SanJose1(config)#enable password cisco

Capetown(config)#isdn switch-type basic-ni
Capetown(config)#username SanJose1 password cisco
Capetown(config)#username jack password cisco
Capetown(config)#enable password cisco
```

On both routers, configure **dialer-list 1** to identify all IP traffic as interesting. The following configuration initiates a dialup session:

```
SanJose1(config)#dialer-list 1 protocol ip permit
```

Step 3

Configure the physical BRI interface on SanJose1 and Capetown to use dialer profiles. Be sure to enter encapsulation configuration commands for both the physical interface (BRI 0/0) and the logical interface, such as dialer0 and so on. Also, remember to use the **dialer pool-member** command as follows to bind the physical BRI interface with the logical dialer interfaces:

```
SanJose1(config)#interface bri0/0
SanJose1(config-if)#isdn spid1 51055510000001 5551000
SanJose1(config-if)#isdn spid2 51055510010001 5551001
SanJose1(config-if)#encapsulation ppp
SanJose1(config-if)#ppp authentication chap
SanJose1(config-if)#ppp chap hostname jack
SanJose1(config-if)#dialer pool-member 1
SanJose1(config-if)#no shutdown

Capetown(config)#interface bri0/0
Capetown(config-if)#isdn spid1 51055520000001 5552000
Capetown(config-if)#isdn spid2 51055520010001 5552001
Capetown(config-if)#encapsulation ppp
Capetown(config-if)#ppp authentication chap
Capetown(config-if)#ppp chap hostname jill
Capetown(config-if)#dialer pool-member 1
Capetown(config-if)#no shutdown
```

Now, the physical BRI interfaces are configured for ISDN.

Next, configure and test Frame Relay connectivity on both routers. The following is an example of the SanJose1 configuration:

```
SanJose1(config-if)#interface serial 0/0
SanJose1(config-if)#encapsulation frame-relay
SanJose1(config-if)#frame-relay map ip 192.168.192.4 104 broadcast
SanJose1(config-if)#ip address 192.168.192.1 255.255.255.0
```

Step 4

Configure dialer profiles for both routers, starting with SanJose1. Create two dialer interfaces for both routers. You configure each dialer interface to support a specific dial backup feature. You configure interface dialer 0 for process switching that enables load balancing. You use interface dialer 1 as the backup interface. The configurations follow:

```
SanJose1(config)#interface dialer 0
SanJose1(config-if)#ip address 172.16.24.1 255.255.255.0
SanJose1(config-if)#dialer pool 1
SanJose1(config-if)#encapsulation ppp
SanJose1(config-if)#ppp authentication chap
SanJose1(config-if)#dialer remote-name Capetown
```

```
SanJose1(config-if)#dialer-group 1
SanJose1(config-if)#dialer string 5552000
SanJose1(config)#interface dialer 1
SanJose1(config-if)#ip address 10.1.1.1 255.255.255.0
SanJose1(config-if)#dialer pool 1
SanJose1(config-if)#encapsulation ppp
SanJose1(config-if)#ppp authentication chap
SanJose1(config-if)#ppp chap hostname jack
SanJose1(config-if)#dialer remote-name jill
SanJose1(config-if)#dialer-group 1
SanJose1(config-if)#dialer string 5552001
```

Now, create two dialer profiles on Capetown that will communicate with SanJose1, as shown in the following:

```
Capetown(config)#interface dialer 0
Capetown(config-if)#ip address 172.16.24.2 255.255.255.0
Capetown(config-if)#dialer pool 1
Capetown(config-if)#encapsulation ppp
Capetown(config-if)#ppp authentication chap
Capetown(config-if)#dialer remote-name SanJose1
Capetown(config-if)#dialer-group 1
Capetown(config-if)#dialer string 5551000
Capetown(config)#interface dialer 1
Capetown(config-if)#ip address 10.1.1.2 255.255.255.0
Capetown(config-if)#dialer pool 1
Capetown(config-if)#encapsulation ppp
Capetown(config-if)#ppp authentication chap
Capetown(config-if)#ppp chap hostname jill
Capetown(config-if)#dialer remote-name jack
Capetown(config-if)#dialer-group 1
Capetown(config-if)#dialer string 5551001
```

Step 5

Configure multiple static routes on SanJose1 to use both dialer interfaces and the serial interface as the exit interface to the Capetown LAN as follows:

```
SanJose1(config)#ip route 192.168.216.0 255.255.255.0 Serial0/0
SanJose1(config)#ip route 192.168.216.0 255.255.255.0 Dialer1
SanJose1(config)#ip route 192.168.216.0 255.255.255.0 Dialer0
```

You must also configure static routes on Capetown, as follows, so that it has a route to reach the SanJose1 LAN:

```
Capetown(config)#ip route 192.168.0.0 255.255.255.0 Serial0/0
Capetown(config)#ip route 192.168.0.0 255.255.255.0 Dialer1
Capetown(config)#ip route 192.168.0.0 255.255.255.0 Dialer0
```

View the following routing table on SanJose1 to verify that both dialer interfaces and the serial interface are used as exit interfaces to the Capetown LAN:

```
SanJose1#show ip route
Codes: C - connected, S - static, I - IGRP, R - RIP, M - mobile, B - BGP
       D - EIGRP, EX - EIGRP external, O - OSPF, IA - OSPF inter area
       N1 - OSPF NSSA external type 1, N2 - OSPF NSSA external type 2
       E1 - OSPF external type 1, E2 - OSPF external type 2, E - EGP
       i - IS-IS, L1 - IS-IS level-1, L2 - IS-IS level-2, ia - IS-IS inter
   area
       * - candidate default, U - per-user static route, o - ODR
       P - periodic downloaded static route
Gateway of last resort is not set
C    192.168.192.0/24 is directly connected, Serial0/0
     172.16.0.0/24 is subnetted, 1 subnets
```

```
C         172.16.24.0 is directly connected, Dialer0
S     192.168.216.0/24 is directly connected, Dialer0
                        is directly connected, Serial0/0
                        is directly connected, Dialer1
      10.0.0.0/24 is subnetted, 1 subnets
C         10.1.1.0 is directly connected, Dialer1
C     192.168.0.0/24 is directly connected, FastEthernet0/0
```

Step 6

Enable process switching on all WAN interfaces on SanJose1. With emerging Layer 3 technologies, you rarely use process switching on a production network. For the purpose of this lab, enter the following to configure SanJose1 to load-balance on a per-packet basis over the point-to-point and the ISDN connection:

```
SanJose1(config)#interface serial 0/0
SanJose1(config-if)#no ip route-cache
SanJose1(config-if)#interface dialer 0
SanJose1(config-if)#no ip route-cache
SanJose1(config-if)#interface dialer 1
SanJose1(config-if)#no ip route-cache
```

When you enable process switching on both dialer interfaces and on the serial interface, half the packets are sent out through the serial interface. The other half of the packets travel over the dialer interfaces. The path selection alternates with each packet received.

Step 7

Make the secondary ISDN link active in case the primary link fails. Issue the following to configure the physical BRI 0/0 interface as a backup interface to Serial0/0 on SanJose1:

```
SanJose1(config)#interface s0/0
SanJose1(config-if)#backup interface dialer 1
SanJose1(config-if)#backup delay 6 8
```

Use the **show ip route** command as follows to examine SanJose1's routing table:

```
SanJose1#show ip route
Codes: C - connected, S - static, I - IGRP, R - RIP, M - mobile, B - BGP
       D - EIGRP, EX - EIGRP external, O - OSPF, IA - OSPF inter area
       N1 - OSPF NSSA external type 1, N2 - OSPF NSSA external type 2
       E1 - OSPF external type 1, E2 - OSPF external type 2, E - EGP
       i - IS-IS, L1 - IS-IS level-1, L2 - IS-IS level-2, ia - IS-IS inter
   area
       * - candidate default, U - per-user static route, o - ODR
       P - periodic downloaded static route
Gateway of last resort is not set
C     192.168.192.0/24 is directly connected, Serial0/0
      172.16.0.0/24 is subnetted, 1 subnets
C         172.16.24.0 is directly connected, Dialer0
S     192.168.216.0/24 is directly connected, Serial0/0
                        is directly connected, Dialer0
C     192.168.0.0/24 is directly connected, FastEthernet0/0
```

Note: The static route that utilizes interface dialer 1 is flushed from the SanJose1 routing table.

Step 8

SanJose1 has two routes to the destination network in the table. Verify that SanJose1 is load-balancing incoming traffic over both primary and secondary links. Observe the load balancing process by using the **debug ip packet** command. The following command outputs information about IP packets sent and received by the router:

```
SanJose1#debug ip packet
```

With the **debug** running, send a few packets from SanJose1 to the Capetown 192.168.216.0 network and observe the output. Notice that the **debug** output shows that IP packets are sent out through the serial 0/0 and dialer 0 interfaces:

```
SanJose1#ping 192.168.216.1
Type escape sequence to abort.
Sending 5, 100-byte ICMP Echos to 192.168.216.1, timeout is 2 seconds:
!!!!!
Success rate is 100 percent (5/5), round-trip min/avg/max = 32/34/36 ms
SanJose1#
IP: s=192.168.192.1 (local), d=192.168.216.1 (Serial0/0), len 100, sending
IP: s=192.168.216.1 (Serial0/0), d=192.168.192.1 (Serial0/0), len 100, rcvd 3
IP: s=192.168.192.1 (local), d=192.168.216.1 (Dialer0), len 100, sending
IP: s=192.168.216.1 (Serial0/0), d=192.168.192.1 (Serial0/0), len 100, rcvd 3
IP: s=192.168.192.1 (local), d=192.168.216.1 (Serial0/0), len 100, sending
IP: s=192.168.216.1 (Serial0/0), d=192.168.192.1 (Serial0/0), len 100, rcvd 3
IP: s=192.168.192.1 (local), d=192.168.216.1 (Dialer0), len 100, sending
IP: s=192.168.216.1 (Serial0/0), d=192.168.192.1 (Serial0/0), len 100, rcvd 3
IP: s=192.168.192.1 (local), d=192.168.216.1 (Serial0/0), len 100, sending
IP: s=192.168.216.1 (Serial0/0), d=192.168.192.1 (Serial0/0), len 100, rcvd 3
```

Step 9

Prior to testing the backup configuration, use the **debug backup** command as follows to monitor the backup process on SanJose1:

```
SanJose1#debug backup
Backup events debugging is on
```

To test dial backup with dialer profiles, unplug the serial cable on both routers. Notice the **debug** output on SanJose1. The following shows that interface dialer 1 has changed its state from a backup passive mode to an active state:

```
%LINEPROTO-5-UPDOWN: Line protocol on Interface Serial0/0,changed state to
  down
BACKUP(Serial0/0): event = primary went down
BACKUP(Serial0/0): changed state to "waiting to backup"
BACKUP(Serial0/0): event = timer expired
BACKUP(Serial0/0): secondary interface (Dialer1) made active
BACKUP(Serial0/0): changed state to "backup mode"
%LINK-3-UPDOWN: Interface Dialer1, changed state to up
BACKUP(Dialer1): event = primary came up
```

Step 10

Interface dialer 1 has become the primary link. Verify that SanJose1 is load balancing between the dialer 0 interface and dialer 1 interface. With the **debug ip packet** command still enabled on SanJose1, ping 192.168.216.1 from SanJose1 as follows:

```
SanJose1#ping 192.168.216.1
Type escape sequence to abort.
Sending 5, 100-byte ICMP Echos to 192.168.216.1, timeout is 2 seconds:
!!!!!
Success rate is 100 percent (5/5), round-trip min/avg/max = 32/33/36 ms
SanJose1#
07:03:27: IP: s=10.1.1.1 (local), d=192.168.216.1 (Dialer1), len 100, sending
07:03:27: IP: s=192.168.216.1 (Dialer1), d=10.1.1.1 (Dialer1), len 100, rcvd 3
07:03:27: IP: s=10.1.1.1 (local), d=192.168.216.1 (Dialer0), len 100, sending
```

```
07:03:27: IP: s=192.168.216.1 (Dialer1), d=10.1.1.1 (Dialer1), len 100, rcvd 3
07:03:27: IP: s=10.1.1.1 (local), d=192.168.216.1 (Dialer1), len 100, sending
07:03:28: IP: s=192.168.216.1 (Dialer1), d=10.1.1.1 (Dialer1), len 100, rcvd 3
07:03:28: IP: s=10.1.1.1 (local), d=192.168.216.1 (Dialer0), len 100, sending
07:03:28: IP: s=192.168.216.1 (Dialer1), d=10.1.1.1 (Dialer1), len 100, rcvd 3
07:03:28: IP: s=10.1.1.1 (local), d=192.168.216.1 (Dialer1), len 100, sending
07:03:28: IP: s=192.168.216.1 (Dialer1), d=10.1.1.1 (Dialer1), len 100, rcvd 3
```

From the **debug** output, you can see that packet flow from SanJose1 is sent out the dialer 0 interface and dialer 1 interface.

Lab 8.7.4: Configuring DDR Backup Using BRIs and Dialer Watch

Estimated Time: 45 Minutes

Objective

In this lab, you configure ISDN physical BRI interface for dialer watch. Figure 8-4 shows the sample topology in this lab.

Figure 8-4   Sample Topology for Lab 8.7.4

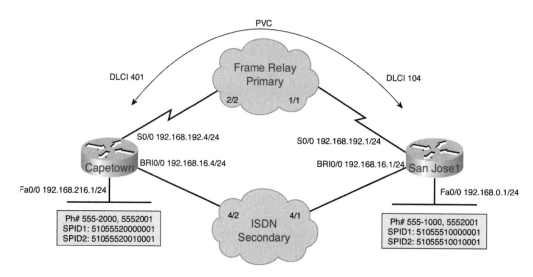

Equipment Requirements

This lab requires two routers, two hosts, and an Adtran or similar device, configured as shown in Figure 8-4.

Scenario

The International Travel Agency asked you to back up the primary route to the SanJose1 LAN. It has asked you to configure dialer watch on its Capetown router to monitor dynamic Enhanced Interior Gateway Routing Protocol (EIGRP) routes to the SanJose1 LAN.

Step 1

Build the network as shown in Figure 8-4. If using the Atlas 550 as a WAN emulator, be sure to use the ports as indicated in the figure. Before beginning this lab, reload each router after erasing its startup configuration. This step prevents problems that residual configurations might cause.

Step 2

Configure both routers to use the appropriate ISDN switch type, National ISDN-1. You use PPP encapsulation and CHAP authentication on the B channels. Therefore, enter the case-sensitive username and password information on both routers, as follows:

```
SanJose1(config)#isdn switch-type basic-ni
SanJose1(config)#username Capetown password cisco
SanJose1(config)#enable password cisco
```

```
Capetown(config)#isdn switch-type basic-ni
Capetown(config)#username SanJose1 password cisco
Capetown(config)#enable password cisco
```

On both routers, configure **dialer-list 1** as follows to use an extended access list to identify interesting traffic that will initiate a DDR session:

```
SanJose1(config)#dialer-list 1 protocol ip list 101
SanJose1(config)#access-list 101 deny eigrp any any
SanJose1(config)#access-list 101 permit ip any any
```

The first access-list deny statement marks all EIGRP packets as uninteresting. This step prevents EIGRP updates from keeping the secondary link up.

Step 3

Configure and test ISDN BRI on Capetown as follows:

```
Capetown(config)#interface bri 0/0
Capetown(config-if)#ip address 192.168.16.4 255.255.255.0
Capetown(config-if)#encapsulation ppp
Capetown(config-if)#ppp authentication chap
Capetown(config-if)#isdn spid1 51055520000001 5552000
Capetown(config-if)#isdn spid2 51055520010001 5552001
Capetown(config-if)#dialer map ip 192.168.16.1 name SanJose1 broadcast
  5551000
Capetown(config-if)#dialer idle-timeout 60
Capetown(config-if)#dialer-group 1
```

Next, enter the following to configure SanJose1:

```
SanJose1(config)#interface bri 0/0
SanJose1(config-if)#ip address 192.168.16.1 255.255.255.0
SanJose1(config-if)#encapsulation ppp
SanJose1(config-if)#ppp authentication chap
SanJose1(config-if)#isdn spid1 51055510000001 5551000
SanJose1(config-if)#isdn spid2 51055510010001 5551001
SanJose1(config-if)#dialer map ip 192.168.16.4 name Capetown broadcast
SanJose1(config-if)#dialer idle-timeout 60
SanJose1(config-if)#dialer-group 1
```

Note: SanJose1 only accepts BRI calls, so do not configure a phone number with the **dialer map** statement.

Ping across the ISDN link from Capetown to the SanJose1 192.168.16.1 LAN. The ping should be successful. Troubleshoot as necessary.

Step 4

Configure and test Frame Relay connectivity on both routers. The Capetown configuration appears here as an example:

```
Capetown(config)#interface s0/0
Capetown(config-if)#ip address 192.168.192.4 255.255.255.0
Capetown(config-if)#encapsulation frame-relay
Capetown(config-if)#frame-relay map ip 192.168.192.1 401 broadcast
```

After you verify that the Frame Relay link is operational between SanJose1 and Capetown, use EIGRP on both routers and enable updates on all active interfaces. The Capetown configuration appears here as an example:

```
Capetown(config)#router eigrp 100
Capetown(config-router)#network 192.168.192.0
```

```
Capetown(config-router)#network 192.168.16.0
Capetown(config-router)#network 192.168.216.0
```

Use the **ping** command to verify connectivity between all interfaces. Troubleshoot as necessary.

Use the **show ip route** command as follows to verify the Capetown routing table:

```
Capetown#show ip route
Codes: C - connected, S - static, I - IGRP, R - RIP, M - mobile, B - BGP
       D - EIGRP, EX - EIGRP external, O - OSPF, IA - OSPF inter area
       N1 - OSPF NSSA external type 1, N2 - OSPF NSSA external type 2
       E1 - OSPF external type 1, E2 - OSPF external type 2, E - EGP
       i - IS-IS, L1 -IS-IS level-1, L2 - IS-IS level-2, ia - IS-IS inter
   area
          * - candidate default, U - per-user static route, o - ODR
          P - periodic downloaded static route
Gateway of last resort is not set
C    192.168.192.0/24 is directly connected, Serial0/0
C    192.168.216.0/24 is directly connected, FastEthernet0/0
D    192.168.0.0/24 [90/2172416] via 192.168.192.1, 00:01:15, Serial0/0
C    192.168.16.0/24 is directly connected, BRI0/0
```

1. According to the output, what route is Capetown using to reach the 192.168.0.0 network?

_____

_____

Step 5

Configure dialer watch to immediately initiate a dialup session when the primary link goes down. When the primary link goes down, the EIGRP routing protocol immediately notifies the dialer-watch–enabled router to bring up the secondary link.

Define the network the dialer-watch– enabled router is to monitor. Use the following command to watch the SanJose1 LAN:

```
Capetown(config)#dialer watch-list 2 ip 192.168.0.0 255.255.255.0
```

Next, enable dialer watch on the Capetown BRI interface using the following command:

```
Capetown(config)#interface bri0/0
Capetown(config-if)#dialer watch-group 2
Capetown(config-if)#dialer watch-disable 15
```

The watch group number tells Capetown to watch the route specified with the **dialer watch-list 2** statement. The optional **dialer watch-disable** command sets the disable timer on the backup interface. This setting delays disconnecting the backup interface for the set number of seconds after the primary interface becomes active.

Step 6

To complete the dialer watch configuration, create a dialer map statement as follows, for the network specified by **dialer watch-list 2** :

```
Capetown(config)#interface bri0/0
Capetown(config-if)#dialer map ip 192.168.0.0 name SanJose1 broadcast 5551000
Capetown(config-if)#dialer map ip 192.168.0.0 name SanJose1 broadcast 5551001
```

The dialer map statement specifies the network being watched by the **dialer watch-list** command. When the "watched route" disappears, the Capetown router knows to dial the specified number to reach the lost network.

Step 7

Test the **dial watch** configuration by unplugging the serial cable from Capetown. Wait for a few seconds and then verify the Capetown routing table as follows:

```
Capetown#show ip route
Codes: C - connected, S - static, I - IGRP, R - RIP, M - mobile, B - BGP
       D - EIGRP, EX - EIGRP external, O - OSPF, IA - OSPF inter area
       N1 - OSPF NSSA external type 1, N2 - OSPF NSSA external type 2
       E1 - OSPF external type 1, E2 - OSPF external type 2, E - EGP
       i - IS-IS, L1 - IS-IS level-1, L2 - IS-IS level-2, ia -IS-IS inter area
       * - candidate default, U - per-user static route, o - ODR
       P - periodic downloaded static route
Gateway of last resort is not set
D    192.168.192.0/24 [90/41024000] via 192.168.16.1, 03:36:57, BRI0/0
C    192.168.216.0/24 is directly connected, FastEthernet0/0
     192.168.0.0/24 is variably subnetted, 2 subnets, 2 masks
C       192.168.0.0/32 is directly connected, BRI0/0
D       192.168.0.0/24 [90/40514560] via 192.168.16.1, 03:37:23, BRI0/0
C    192.168.16.0/24 is directly connected, BRI0/0
```

The backup link is activated. Notice that the SanJose1 192.168.192.0 network is installed in the Capetown routing table using the backup link BRI 0/0.

You can also use the **show dialer** command to verify that the DDR interface is activated by dialing on a watched route loss, as shown in the following:

```
Capetown#show dialer
BRI0/0 - dialer type = ISDN
Dial String      Successes    Failures    Last DNIS    Last status
5551001                  0           0    never                 -
5551000                221           0    00:00:49     successful
0 incoming call(s) have been screened.
0 incoming call(s) rejected for callback.

BRI0/0:1 - dialer type = ISDN
Idle timer (60 secs), Fast idle timer (20 secs)
Wait for carrier (30 secs), Re-enable (15 secs)
Dialer state is data link layer up
Dial reason: Dialing on watched route loss
Time until disconnect 57 secs
Connected to 5551000 (SanJose1)

BRI0/0:2 - dialer type = ISDN
Idle timer (60 secs), Fast idle timer (20 secs)
Wait for carrier (30 secs), Re-enable (15 secs)
Dialer state is idle
```

Chapter 9

Managing Network Performance with Queuing and Compression

Lab 9.8.1: Managing Network Performance Using Class-Based Weighted Fair Queuing (CBWFQ) and Low Latency Queuing (LLQ)

Estimated Time: 45 Minutes

Objective

In this lab, you use an access list to define the traffic of interest that is to be classified and configure a class map that associates the access list to a content class. Configure a policy map that associates a content class to a queue and guarantees bandwidth. Configure class-based weighted fair queuing (CBWFQ) on an interface and verify its operation. Configure low latency queuing (LLQ) on an interface and verify its operation. Figure 9-1 shows the sample topology for this lab.

Figure 9-1   Sample Topology for Lab 9.8.1

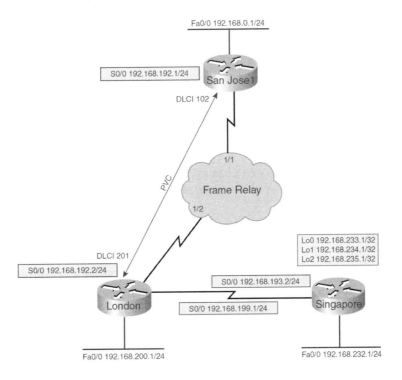

Equipment Requirements

This lab requires three routers configured as shown in Figure 9-1. Note that you cannot use a 2500 series router for this lab.

Scenario

Users at the London office of the International Travel Agency are reporting problems with traffic coming from the SanJose1 site. The network link is dropping HTTP packets because of other network traffic on the Frame Relay link. Users at the SanJose1 office are also complaining that Telnet traffic going to the London office is also being degraded.

After studying traffic patterns, International Travel Agency management has decided to allocate 50 percent of the available Frame Relay bandwidth for HTTP network traffic going to the London office from the SanJose1 office LAN connection. Another 25 percent of all network traffic traversing the Frame Relay link will be allocated to Telnet traffic coming from the SanJose1 LAN connection. All other traffic will contend for the remaining available Frame Relay bandwidth.

International Travel Agency has decided to implement CBWFQ to support the management-defined quality of service (QoS) requirements.

The Singapore site is directly connected to the London site. You use the Singapore router to generate IP traffic to test the queuing on the Frame Relay connection. You configure three loopback interfaces on the Singapore router for the extended ping tests.

Step 1

Before beginning this lab, reload each router after erasing its startup configuration. Taking this step prevents problems that residual configurations might cause. Cable the network according to Figure 9-1. This lab assumes that you use an Adtran Atlas 550 to emulate the Frame Relay cloud. Be sure to connect the serial interfaces on the router to the port as labeled in the figure. On each router, configure its respective host name and Fast Ethernet address.

On the SanJose1 router, configure the following:

```
SanJose1(config)#interface serial0/0
SanJose1(config-if)#ip address 192.168.192.1 255.255.255.0
SanJose1(config-if)#encapsulation frame-relay
SanJose1(config-if)#frame-relay lmi-type ansi
SanJose1(config-if)#no shutdown
```

For convenience, configure a default route to London as follows:

```
SanJose1(config)#ip route 0.0.0.0 0.0.0.0 192.168.192.2
```

On the London router, configure the serial interfaces and static routes as follows:

```
London(config)#interface serial0/0
London(config-if)#ip address 192.168.192.2 255.255.255.0
London(config-if)#encapsulation frame-relay
London(config-if)#frame-relay lmi-type ansi
London(config-if)#no shutdown
London(config-if)#exit

London(config)#interface serial0/1
London(config-if)#ip address 192.168.199.1 255.255.255.0
London(config-if)#no shutdown
London(config-if)#exit

London(config)#ip route 192.168.0.0 255.255.255.0 192.168.192.1
London(config)#ip route 192.168.232.0 255.255.248.0 192.168.199.2
```

On the Singapore router, configure the serial interface and enable password, Telnet services, loopback interfaces, and the default route as follows:

```
Singapore(config)#interface serial0/0
Singapore(config-if)#ip address 192.168.199.2 255.255.255.0
Singapore(config-if)#clock rate 56000
Singapore(config-if)#no shutdown
Singapore(config-if)#exit

Singapore(config)#interface lo 0
Singapore(config-if)#ip address 192.168.233.1 255.255.255.255
Singapore(config)#interface lo 1
Singapore(config-if)#ip address 192.168.234.1 255.255.255.255
Singapore(config)#interface lo 2
Singapore(config-if)#ip address 192.168.235.1 255.255.255.255

Singapore(config)#enable password cisco
Singapore(config)#line vty 0 4
Singapore(config)#password cisco
Singapore(config)#login
Singapore(config)#ip route 0.0.0.0 0.0.0.0 192.168.199.1
```

With the extended **ping** command, verify connectivity between the Fast Ethernet LAN on SanJose1 and the Fast Ethernet LAN and loopback addresses on Singapore.

Step 2

In this step, you configure the class map and policy map for CBWFQ on the SanJose1 router. On the SanJose1 router, create an extended IP access list 100 to permit HTTP traffic requests coming from the SanJose1 LAN going to the London LAN:

```
SanJose1(config)#access-list 100 permit tcp 192.168.0.0 0.0.0.255
192.168.200.0 0.0.0.255 eq www
```

Create another extended IP access list 101 to permit Telnet traffic requests originating from the SanJose1 LAN going to London LAN:

```
SanJose1(config)#access-list 101 permit tcp 192.168.0.0 0.0.0.255
192.168.200.0 0.0.0.255 eq telnet
```

Create a class map named HTTP-CLASS and configure a match condition with access list 100, as follows:

```
SanJose1(config)#class-map match-all HTTP-CLASS
SanJose1(config-cmap)#match access-group 100
```

Create a class map named TELNET-CLASS and configure a match condition with access list 101:

```
SanJose1(config-cmap)#class-map match-all TELNET-CLASS
SanJose1(config-cmap)#match access-group 101
SanJose1(config-cmap)#exit
```

Create a policy map named CBWFQ-CENTRAL. In the policy map, create a traffic policy for class HTTP-CLASS to allocate a minimum of 50 percent of the available bandwidth. Under the same policy map, create a traffic policy for class TELNET-CLASS, allocating a minimum of 25 percent of the available bandwidth:

```
SanJose1(config)#policy-map CBWFQ-CENTRAL
SanJose1(config-pmap)#class HTTP-CLASS
SanJose1(config-pmap-c)#bandwidth percent 50
```

```
SanJose1(config-pmap-c)#class TELNET-CLASS
SanJose1(config-pmap-c)#bandwidth percent 25
SanJose1(config-pmap-c)#exit
```

Create a Frame Relay traffic shaping map class called TSLAB. Set the committed information rate (CIR) to 9600, the traffic rate to 9600, and the adaptive shaping to backward explicit congestion notification (BECN). Finally, apply the service policy CBWFQ-CENTRAL as follows:

```
SanJose1(config)#map-class frame-relay TSLAB
SanJose1(config-map-class)#frame-relay cir 9600
SanJose1(config-map-class)#frame-relay traffic-rate 9600 9600
SanJose1(config-map-class)#frame-relay adaptive-shaping becn
SanJose1(config-map-class)#service-policy output CBWFQ-CENTRAL
SanJose1(config-map-class)#exit
```

Enable Frame Relay traffic shaping on the S0/0 interface and configure the interface to use the Frame Relay class TSLAB as follows:

```
SanJose1(config)#interface serial0/0
SanJose1(config-if)#frame-relay class TSLAB
SanJose1(config-if)#frame-relay traffic-shaping
```

Verify the CBWFQ configuration on the SanJose1 router as follows:

```
SanJose1#show policy-map int
 Serial0/0: DLCI 102 -

  Service-policy output: CBWFQ-CENTRAL

    Class-map: HTTP-CLASS (match-all)
      0 packets, 0 bytes
      5 minute offered rate 0 bps, drop rate 0 bps
      Match: access-group 100
      Queueing
        Output Queue: Conversation 25
        Bandwidth 50 (%) Max Threshold 64 (packets)
        (pkts matched/bytes matched) 0/0
        (depth/total drops/no-buffer drops) 0/0/0

    Class-map: TELNET-CLASS (match-all)
      0 packets, 0 bytes
      5 minute offered rate 0 bps, drop rate 0 bps
      Match: access-group 101
      Queueing
        Output Queue: Conversation 26
        Bandwidth 25 (%) Max Threshold 64 (packets)
        (pkts matched/bytes matched) 0/0
        (depth/total drops/no-buffer drops) 0/0/0

    Class-map: class-default (match-any)
      0 packets, 0 bytes
      5 minute offered rate 0 bps, drop rate 0 bps
      Match: any
```

Verify that CBWFQ is applied correctly to the Frame Relay interface as follows:

```
SanJose1#show frame-relay pvc 102

PVC Statistics for interface Serial0/0 (Frame Relay DTE)

DLCI = 102, DLCI USAGE = LOCAL, PVC STATUS = ACTIVE, INTERFACE = Serial0/0

  input pkts 12           output pkts 10           in bytes 1108
```

```
 out bytes 1040          dropped pkts 0          in pkts dropped 0
 out pkts dropped 0           out bytes dropped 0
 in FECN pkts 0          in BECN pkts 0          out FECN pkts 0
 out BECN pkts 0         in DE pkts 0            out DE pkts 0
 out bcast pkts 0        out bcast bytes 0
 Shaping adapts to BECN
 pvc create time 00:18:05, last time pvc status changed 00:15:47
 cir 9600        bc 9600       be 0          byte limit 150    interval 125
 mincir 4800       byte increment 150   Adaptive Shaping BECN
 pkts 0          bytes 0         pkts delayed 0         bytes delayed 0
 shaping inactive
 traffic shaping drops 0
 service policy CBWFQ-CENTRAL
Serial0/0: DLCI 102 -

 Service-policy output: CBWFQ-CENTRAL
********Output Omitted********
```

Step 3

In this step, you implement LLQ on the London router. On the London router, create an extended IP access list 102 to simulate all low latency traffic such as Voice over IP (VoIP). To do so, the access-list will permit traffic from the Singapore site's loopback 0 interface to SanJose1 site's LAN:

```
London(config)#access-list 102 permit ip host 192.168.233.1  192.168.0.0
   0.0.0.255
```

Create an extended IP access list 103 to permit traffic from the Singapore site's loopback 1 interface to SanJose1 site's LAN:

```
London(config)#access-list 103 permit ip host 192.168.234.1  192.168.0.0
   0.0.0.255
```

Create an extended IP access list 104 to permit traffic from the Singapore site's loopback 2 interface to SanJose1 site's LAN:

```
London(config)#access-list 104 permit ip host 192.168.235.1  192.168.0.0
   0.0.0.255
```

You must create three class maps to match the conditions of the access lists. Create the first class map named LLQ-102-CLASS and configure a match condition with access list 102. Create the second class map named LLQ-103-CLASS and configure a match condition with access list 102. Create the third class map named LLQ-104-CLASS and configure a match condition with access list 102:

```
London(config)#class-map match-all LLQ-102-CLASS
London(config-cmap)#match access-group 102
London(config-cmap)#class-map match-all CBWFQ-103-CLASS
London(config-cmap)#match access-group 103
London(config-cmap)#class-map match-all CBWFQ-104-CLASS
London(config-cmap)#match access-group 104
```

Create a policy map named CBWFQ-LONDON and configure a traffic policy for the class of traffic named LLQ-102-CLASS, specifying a priority of 8 as follows:

```
London(config-pmap)#policy-map CBWFQ-LONDON
London(config-pmap)#class LLQ-102-CLASS
London(config-pmap-c)#priority 8
London(config-pmap-c)#class CBWFQ-103-CLASS
London(config-pmap-c)#bandwidth percent 25
London(config-pmap-c)#class CBWFQ-104-CLASS
London(config-pmap-c)#bandwidth percent 25
```

Create a Frame Relay traffic shaping map class called TSLAB. Set the CIR to 28000, the minimum CIR to 18000, and the adaptive shaping to BECN. Finally, apply the service policy CBWFQ-LONDON as follows:

```
London(config)#map-class frame-relay TSLAB
London(config-map-class)#frame-relay cir 28000
London(config-map-class)#frame-relay mincir 18000
London(config-map-class)#frame-relay adaptive-shaping becn
London(config-map-class)#service-policy output CBWFQ-LONDON
```

Step 4

Verify the CBWFQ/LLQ configuration on the London router as follows:

```
London#show policy-map
  Policy Map CBWFQ-LONDON
    Class LLQ-102-CLASS
      Strict Priority
      Bandwidth 8 (kbps) Burst 200 (Bytes)
    Class CBWFQ-103-CLASS
      Bandwidth 25 (%) Max Threshold 64 (packets)
    Class CBWFQ-104-CLASS
      Bandwidth 25 (%) Max Threshold 64 (packets)
```

Step 5

Generate traffic from the Singapore router to congest the London-to-SanJose1 Frame Relay link.

Establish three connections to the Singapore router to generate significant network traffic. You must do so on all three extended ping sessions in a timely manner to congest the Frame Relay link between the London and SanJose1 sites.

It is very important that you read and understand the following steps before being attempting them:

1.   Establish a console session to the Singapore router.

2.   Execute an extended ping to the SanJose1 router LAN interface using the loopback 0 address as the source address. In addition, use 10,000 as the ping count with a byte size of 60 bytes. This setup simulates a VoIP data flow.

3.   While the extended ping is ongoing, exit the Singapore console connection and console to the SanJose1 router.

4.   Establish a Telnet session to the Singapore router from the SanJose1 router.

5.   Execute an extended ping to the SanJose1 router LAN interface using the loopback 1 address as the source address. In addition, use 10,000 as the ping count with a byte size of 1500 bytes. This setup simulates another IP data flow.

6.   While the extended ping is ongoing, suspend the Telnet session by pressing **Ctrl+Shift+6** twice and then press **X**. This step returns to the prompt on the SanJose1 router.

7.   Establish a second Telnet session into the Singapore router from the SanJose1 router.

8.   Execute an extended ping to the SanJose1 router LAN interface using the loopback 2 address as the source address. In addition, use 10,000 as the ping count with a byte size of 1500 bytes. This setup simulates another IP data flow.

9.   Exit the console session on the SanJose1 router.

10. Enter the London router through the console session.

11. On the London site router, use the **show** commands in the command list to complete the following information:

    Bandwidth allocated to the LLQ-102-CLASS: _____

    Bandwidth allocated to the CBWFQ-103-CLASS: _____

    Bandwidth allocated to the CBWFQ-104-CLASS: _____

    Drop rate for the CBWFQ-103-CLASS: _____

    Drop rate for the CBWFQ-104-CLASS: _____

12. Erase the SanJose1, London, and Singapore router configurations and reload the routers.

Chapter 10

Scaling IP Addresses with NAT

Lab 10.5.1: Configuring Static NAT

Estimated Time: 30 Minutes

Objective

In this lab, you configure network address translation (NAT) static translation to provide reliable outside access to three shared company servers. Figure 10-1 shows the sample topology.

Figure 10-1   Sample Topology for Lab 10.5.1

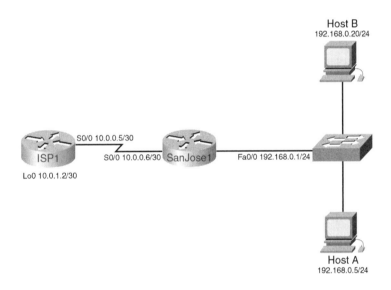

Equipment Requirements

This lab requires two routers configured as shown in Figure 10-1. Note that you cannot use a 2500 series router for this lab.

Scenario

The International Travel Agency has expanded and updated its network. It chose to use the 192.168.0.0 /24 private addresses and NAT to handle connectivity with the outside world. To secure the outside IP addresses from its Internet service provider (ISP), International Travel Agency must pay a monthly fee for each IP address. International Travel Agency has asked you to set up a series of prototypes to test the capabilities of NAT to meet its requirements. The company hopes to be able to get by with 14 real IP addresses, 42.0.0.48 /28. For a variety of reasons, including security concerns, the company wants to hide the internal network from the outside.

Step 1

Build and configure the network according to Figure 10-1. This configuration requires the use of subnet zero. Depending on the version of Cisco IOS, you might need to enter the **ip subnet-zero** command.

Configure SanJose1 to use a default route to ISP1, as shown in the following:

```
SanJose1(config)#ip route 0.0.0.0 0.0.0.0 10.0.0.5
```

Host A represents one of the proposed shared servers that will be part of a Fast Ethernet LAN attached to SanJose1. Host B represents a user in the International Travel Agency network.

Step 2

Verify the configurations with the **show running-config** command.

Verify that SanJose1 can ping to the serial interface for ISP1, 10.0.0.5, and that ISP1 can ping SanJose1's serial interface, 10.0.0.6.

At this time, ISP1 cannot ping either workstation or SanJose1's Fast Ethernet interface, 192.168.0.1.

1. Both workstations can ping each other and 10.0.0.6 but cannot ping 10.0.0.5. Why does the latter ping fail?

In fact, the ping request should be getting to 10.0.0.5. Because ISP1 has no entry in its routing table for the 192.168.0.0 /24 network, ISP1 cannot reply. To solve this problem, you configure a static route in Step 7.

Step 3

SanJose1 is the boundary router where you configure NAT. The router will translate the inside local addresses to inside global addresses. It essentially converts the internal private addresses into legal public addresses for use on the Internet.

On SanJose1, create static translations between the inside local addresses, the servers to be shared, and the inside global addresses using the following commands:

```
SanJose1(config)#ip nat inside source static 192.168.0.3 42.0.0.49
SanJose1(config)#ip nat inside source static 192.168.0.4 42.0.0.50
SanJose1(config)#ip nat inside source static 192.168.0.5 42.0.0.51
```

1. If you need a static translation for a fourth server, 192.168.0.6, what is the appropriate command?

Step 4

Next, enter the following to specify an interface on SanJose1 to be used by inside network hosts requiring address translation:

```
SanJose1(config)#interface fastethernet0/0
SanJose1(config-if)#ip nat inside
```

Enter the following to specify an interface as the outside NAT interface:

```
SanJose1(config)#interface serial0/0
SanJose1(config-if)#ip nat outside
```

Step 5

To see the static translations, use the **show ip nat translations** command. The results should look similar to the following:

```
SanJose1#show ip nat translations
Pro Inside global     Inside local      Outside local     Outside global
--- 42.0.0.49         192.168.0.3       ---               ---
--- 42.0.0.50         192.168.0.4       ---               ---
--- 42.0.0.51         192.168.0.5       ---               ---
```

Use the **show ip nat statistics** command to see what NAT activity has occurred. The results should look similar to the following:

```
SanJose1#show ip nat statistics
Total active translations: 3 (3 static, 0 dynamic; 0 extended)
Outside interfaces:
  Serial0/0
Inside interfaces:
  FastEthernet0/0
Hits: 0  Misses: 0
Expired translations: 0
Dynamic mappings:
```

Notice that the hits value is currently zero (0).

Step 6

From Host A, ping 10.0.0.5, which is ISP1's serial interface. The pings should still fail because ISP1 has no route for 192.168.0.0 /24 in its routing table.

Return to the console connection of SanJose1 and type **show ip nat statistics**, as follows:

```
SanJose1#show ip nat statistics
Total active translations: 3 (3 static, 0 dynamic; 0 extended)
Outside interfaces:
  Serial0/0
Inside interfaces:
  FastEthernet0/0
Hits: 4  Misses: 0
Expired translations: 0
Dynamic mappings:
```

Notice that the hits equal four (4). This number indicates that the translation happened even though the console did not receive a response. Remember that the ping replies are not sent because ISP1 does not have a route back to SanJose1.

Step 7

On ISP1, configure the following static route to the global addresses used by SanJose1 for NAT:

```
ISP1(config)#ip route 42.0.0.48 255.255.255.240 10.0.0.6
```

The subnet mask defines the pool of IP addresses as 42.0.0.48 /28.

A ping to 42.0.0.51 should now be successful. This address is the translated address of the shared server, 192.168.0.5.

The **show ip route** command confirms that the static route is present, as the following shows:

```
ISP1#show ip route
Codes: C - connected, S - static, I - IGRP, R - RIP, M - mobile, B - BGP
       D - EIGRP, EX - EIGRP external, O - OSPF, IA - OSPF inter area
       N1 - OSPF NSSA external type 1, N2 - OSPF NSSA external type 2
```

```
        E1 - OSPF external type 1, E2 - OSPF external type 2, E - EGP
        i - IS-IS, L1 - IS-IS level-1, L2 - IS-IS level-2, ia - IS-IS inter
   area
        * - candidate default, U - per-user static route, o - ODR
        P - periodic downloaded static route
Gateway of last resort is not set
     42.0.0.0/28 is subnetted, 1 subnets
S       42.0.0.48 [1/0] via 10.0.0.6
     10.0.0.0/30 is subnetted, 2 subnets
C       10.0.1.0 is directly connected, Loopback0/0
C       10.0.0.4 is directly connected, Serial0/0
```

Step 8

From Host A, ping the ISP1 router at 10.0.0.5. This ping should now be successful.

A ping to the loopback address for ISP1, 10.0.1.2, should be successful as well.

From the console connection to SanJose1, issue the **show ip nat statistics** command and look over the statistics. The number of hits should be much larger than before.

Try the **show ip nat translations verbose** command. The results should look similar to this:

```
SanJose1#show ip nat translations verbose
Pro Inside global     Inside local      Outside local      Outside global
--- 42.0.0.49         192.168.0.3       ---                ---
    create 00:40:25, use 00:40:25,
    flags:
static, use_count: 0
--- 42.0.0.50         192.168.0.4       ---                ---
    create 00:40:25, use 00:40:25,
    flags:
static, use_count: 0
--- 42.0.0.51         192.168.0.5       ---                ---
    create 00:40:25, use 00:06:46,
    flags:
static, use_count: 0
```

Note: The verbose option includes information about how recently each translation was used.

Step 9

From SanJose1, use the **show ip nat statistics** command and note the number of hits.

From Host B, ping both 10.0.0.5 and 10.0.1.2.

1.   Both pings should fail. Why?

_____

From SanJose1, issue the **show ip nat statistics** command again and notice that the number of hits has not changed. The problem is that NAT did not translate Host B's IP address, 192.168.0.20, to one of the global addresses. You can confirm this information with the **show ip nat translations** command.

There is no static translation set up for Host B, which represents a LAN user. You could quickly configure a static translation for this single end user. However, configuring a static translation for every user on the LAN could be a huge task, resulting in hundreds of configuration commands. Dynamic NAT lets you configure the router to assign global addresses dynamically, on an as-needed basis. Whereas static translation might be appropriate for servers, you almost always use dynamic translation with end-user stations. The next lab discusses dynamic NAT.

Lab 10.5.2: Configuring Dynamic NAT

Estimated Time: 30 Minutes

Objective

In this lab, you configure dynamic NAT to provide privately addressed users with access to outside resources. Figure 10-2 shows the sample topology.

Figure 10-2   Sample Topology for 10.5.2

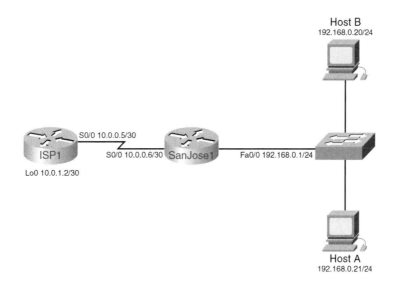

Equipment Requirements

This lab requires that you configure two routers as shown in Figure 10-2. Note that you cannot use a 2500 series router for this lab.

Scenario

The International Travel Agency has expanded and updated its network. It chose to use the 192.168.0.0 /24 private addresses and NAT to handle connectivity with the outside world. In securing the outside IP addresses from its ISP, International Travel Agency has to pay a monthly fee for each IP address. International Travel Agency has asked you to set up a series of prototypes to test the capabilities of NAT to meet its requirements. The company hopes to be able to get by with 14 real IP addresses, 42.0.0.48 /28. For a variety of reasons, including security concerns, the company wants to hide the internal network from the outside.

International Travel Agency is hoping to limit user access to the Internet and other outside resources by limiting the number of connections. You need to prototype basic dynamic translation to see whether it meets International Travel Agency objectives.

Step 1

Build and configure the network according to the Figure 10-2. This configuration requires the use of subnet zero. Depending on the Cisco IOS version, you might need to enter the **ip subnet-zero** command. Both Host A and Host B represent users on the International Travel Agency network.

Enter the following to configure SanJose1 to use a default route to ISP1:

```
SanJose1(config)#ip route 0.0.0.0 0.0.0.0 10.0.0.5
```

On ISP1, configure a static route to the global addresses used by SanJose1 for NAT as follows:

```
ISP1(config)#ip route 42.0.0.48 255.255.255.240 10.0.0.6
```

Step 2

Define a pool of global addresses to be allocated by the dynamic NAT process. Issue the following command on SanJose1:

```
SanJose1(config)#ip nat pool MYNATPOOL 42.0.0.55 42.0.0.55 netmask
  255.255.255.240
```

The name MYNATPOOL is the name of the address pool. If you prefer, you can use a different word. The first 42.0.0.55 in the command is the first IP address in the pool. The second 42.0.0.55 is the last IP address in the pool. This command creates a pool that contains only a single address. Typically, you configure a larger range of addresses in a pool. However, at this time, you use only one address.

Next, configure a standard access list to define which internal source addresses can be translated. Because any users on the International Travel Agency network are being translated, use the following command:

```
SanJose1(config)#access-list 2 permit 192.168.0.0 0.0.0.255
```

To establish the dynamic source translation, link the access list to the name of the NAT pool, as shown in the following:

```
SanJose1(config)#ip nat inside source list 2 pool MYNATPOOL
```

Finally, specify an interface on SanJose1 to be used by inside network hosts requiring address translation:

```
SanJose1(config)#interface fastethernet0/0
SanJose1(config-if)#ip nat inside
```

Also, specify an interface as the outside NAT interface as follows:

```
SanJose1(config)#interface serial0/0
SanJose1(config-if)#ip nat outside
```

Step 3

On SanJose1, enter the **show ip nat translations** command. This step should result in no output. Static translations are permanent and always remain in the translations table. Dynamic translations are only assigned as needed and only appear when active.

From Host A, ping the serial and loopback IP addresses on ISP1. Both pings should work. Troubleshoot as necessary.

Issue the **show ip nat translations** command on SanJose1 again. You should receive a single translation for that workstation. The result might be similar to the following:

```
SanJose1#show ip nat translations
Pro Inside global     Inside local      Outside local     Outside global
--- 42.0.0.55         192.168.0.21      ---               ---
```

From Host B, ping the serial and loopback IP addresses on ISP1. Both pings should fail. The one available IP address in the pool is being used by the other workstation. If you had assigned a larger pool of addresses, Host B could be assigned an address from the pool.

Step 4

Issue the **show ip nat translations verbose** command as follows and examine the output:

```
SanJose1#show ip nat translations verbose
Pro Inside global       Inside local       Outside local      Outside global
--- 42.0.0.55           192.168.0.21       ---                ---
    create 00:13:18, use 00:13:06, left 23:46:53,
    flags: none, use_count: 0
```

1.   According to the output of this command, how much time is left before the dynamic translation times out?

The default timeout value for dynamic NAT translations is 24 hours. The second workstation must wait until the next day before it can be assigned the address.

Next, issue the **show ip nat statistics** command. Notice that it summarizes the translation information, shows the pool of global addresses, and indicates that only one address has been allocated or translated, shown as follows:

```
SanJose1#show ip nat statistics
Total active translations: 1 (0 static, 1 dynamic; 0 extended)
Outside interfaces:
  Serial0/0
Inside interfaces:
  FastEthernet0/0
Hits: 45  Misses: 0
Expired translations: 0
Dynamic mappings:
-- Inside Source
access-list 2 pool MYNATPOOL refcount 1
 pool MYNATPOOL: netmask 255.255.255.240
       start 42.0.0.55 end 42.0.0.55
            type generic, total addresses 1, allocated 1 (100%), misses 4
```

To change the default NAT timeout value from 24 hours, or 86,400 seconds, to 120 seconds, issue the following command:

```
SanJose1(config)#ip nat translation timeout 120
```

You must clear the existing address allocation before the new timer can take effect. To immediately clear the translation table, type **clear ip nat translation *** .

Now, from Host B, ping either interface of ISP1 again. The ping should be successful.

Use the **show ip nat translations** and **show ip nat translations verbose** commands to confirm the translation and to see that the new translations expire in 2 minutes.

Next, perform a ping from Host B and issue the **show ip nat translations verbose** command again. This step shows that the "time left" timer has been reset. Additional hosts will not be allocated an address until a translation has been inactive for the timeout period.

Step 5

In this step, clear the IP NAT translations and configure the NAT pool to include a larger range of global addresses from the pool available to International Travel Agency. Issue the following command on SanJose1:

```
SanJose1(config)#ip nat pool MYNATPOOL 42.0.0.55 42.0.0.62 netmask
  255.255.255.240
```

This command redefines MYNATPOOL to include a range of eight addresses. Both workstations should now be able to ping ISP1.

The **show ip nat translations** command confirms that two translations have occurred, shown as follows:

```
SanJose1#show ip nat translations
Pro Inside global     Inside local      Outside local        Outside global
--- 42.0.0.55         192.168.0.20      ---                  ---
--- 42.0.0.56         192.168.0.21      ---                  ---
```

Increasing the address range in the pool allows more hosts to be translated. However, if every address in the pool is allocated, the timeout period must expire before any other hosts can be allocated an address. As shown in Step 4, an allocated address cannot be released until its host is inactive for the duration of the timeout period.

The next lab shows how to use many-to-one NAT, or NAT overload. An overload configuration can allow hundreds of hosts to use a handful of global addresses, without hosts waiting for timeouts.

Lab 10.5.3: Configuring NAT Overload

Estimated Time: 45 Minutes

Objective

In this lab, you configure dynamic NAT with overload. Figure 10-3 shows the sample topology.

Figure 10-3   Sample Topology for Lab 10.5.3

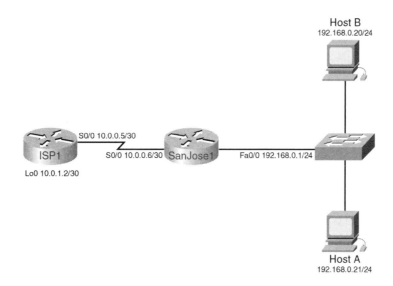

Equipment Requirements

This lab requires two routers configured as shown in Figure 10-3. Note that you cannot use a 2500 series router for this lab.

Scenario

The International Travel Agency expanded and updated its network. It chose to use the 192.168.0.0 /24 private addresses and NAT to handle connectivity with the outside world. In securing the outside IP addresses from their ISP, International Travel Agency has to pay a monthly fee for each IP address. International Travel Agency has asked you to set up a series of prototypes to test the capabilities of NAT to meet its requirements. The company hopes to be able to get by with 14 real IP addresses, 42.0.0.48 /28. For a variety of reasons, including security concerns, the company wants to hide the internal network from the outside.

It appears that the basic dynamic NAT translations are too limiting and cumbersome to meet International Travel Agency needs. Therefore, you must modify the prototype to use the overload feature.

Step 1

Build and configure the network according to Figure 10-3. Depending on the Cisco IOS version, you might need to enter the **ip subnet-zero** command. Both Host A and Host B represent users on the International Travel Agency network.

Enter the following to configure SanJose1 to use a default route to ISP1:

```
SanJose1(config)#ip route 0.0.0.0 0.0.0.0 10.0.0.5
```

On ISP1, enter the following to configure a static route to the global addresses used by SanJose1 for NAT:

```
ISP1(config)#ip route 42.0.0.48 255.255.255.240 10.0.0.6
```

Define a pool of global addresses to be allocated by the dynamic NAT process. Issue the following command on SanJose1:

```
SanJose1(config)#ip nat pool MYNATPOOL 42.0.0.55 42.0.0.62 netmask
  255.255.255.240
```

Configure a standard access list to define which internal source addresses can be translated. Because all users are being translated on the International Travel Agency network, use the following command:

```
SanJose1(config)#access-list 2 permit 192.168.0.0 0.0.0.255
```

Enter the following to specify an interface on SanJose1 to be used by inside network hosts requiring address translation:

```
SanJose1(config)#interface fastethernet0/0
SanJose1(config-if)#ip nat inside
```

Also, enter the following to specify an interface as the outside NAT interface:

```
SanJose1(config)#interface serial0/0
SanJose1(config-if)#ip nat outside
```

Step 2

In Step 1, you created a pool of "real" global IP addresses. The network uses these addresses to provide internally addressed hosts with access to the Internet and other outside resources. However, in the previous implementation, it could allocate each global address to only one host at a time.

The most powerful feature of NAT is address overloading, or port address translation (PAT). Overloading allows multiple inside addresses to map to a single global address. With PAT, literally hundreds of privately addressed nodes can access the Internet using only one global address. The NAT router keeps track of the different conversations by mapping TCP and User Datagram Protocol (UDP) port numbers.

Configure address overloading on SanJose1 with the following command:

```
SanJose1(config)#ip nat inside source list 2 pool MYNATPOOL overload
```

After the overload feature is configured, ping both interfaces of ISP1, 10.0.1.2 and 10.0.0.5, from Host A. The pings should be successful. Next, issue the **show ip nat translations** command as follows:

```
SanJose1#show ip nat translations
Pro Inside global      Inside local      Outside local      Outside global
icmp 42.0.0.55:1536    192.168.0.21:1536 10.0.0.5:1536      10.0.0.5:1536
icmp 42.0.0.55:1536    192.168.0.21:1536 10.0.1.2:1536      10.0.1.2:1536
```

1. What port number is the source of the ping?

    _____

2. What port number is the destination of the ping?

    _____

In addition to tracking the IP addresses translated, the translations table also records the port numbers. Also notice that the first column "Pro" shows the protocol.

Look at the following output from the **show ip nat translations verbose** command:

```
SanJose1#show ip nat translations verbose
Pro Inside global      Inside local      Outside local      Outside global
icmp 42.0.0.55:1536    192.168.0.21:1536 10.0.0.5:1536      10.0.0.5:1536
     create 00:00:09, use 00:00:06, left 00:00:53,
     flags:
extended, use_count: 0
icmp 42.0.0.55:1536    192.168.0.21:1536 10.0.1.2:1536      10.0.1.2:1536
     create 00:00:04, use 00:00:01, left 00:00:58,
     flags:
extended, use_count: 0
```

Note: The timeout for these overloaded dynamic translations of Internet Control Message Protocol (ICMP) is 60 seconds. Also, notice that there is a timeout timer for each session. New activity only resets the time for that session. You might need another ping to see the result on the router.

From the MS-DOS prompt of Host A, quickly issue the following commands and then return to the SanJose1 console to issue the **show ip nat translations** command:

```
HostA:\>ping 10.0.0.5
HostA:\>telnet 10.0.0.5
!Do not login. Return to command window
HostA:\>ftp: 10.0.0.5
!It will fail. Do not worry about it
```

Note: To quit the Windows FTP program, type **bye** and press **Enter**.

After you initiate these three sessions, the output of the **show ip nat translations** command should look similar to the following:

```
SanJose1#show ip nat translations
Pro Inside global      Inside local      Outside local      Outside global
icmp 42.0.0.55:1536    192.168.0.21:1536 10.0.0.5:1536      10.0.0.5:1536
tcp 42.0.0.55:1095     192.168.0.21:1095 10.0.0.5:21        10.0.0.5:21
tcp 42.0.0.55:1094     192.168.0.21:1094 10.0.0.5:23        10.0.0.5:23
```

The NAT router has a pool of eight IP addresses to work with. However, it chooses to continue to use the 42.0.0.55 for both workstations. The Cisco IOS continues to overload the first address in the pool until it reaches its maximum and then moves to the second address, and so on.

Step 3

In this step, you examine the timeout values in more detail. From Host A, initiate FTP and HTTP sessions as follows with ISP1 at 10.0.0.5:

```
HostA:\>ftp 10.0.0.5
```

Note: Because ISP1 is not configured as an FTP server or web server, both sessions fail.

To open an HTTP session, type the IP address for ISP1 in the URL field of a web browser window.

After you attempt both FTP and HTTP sessions, use the **show ip nat translations verbose** command. Examine the following time-left entries, as shown:

```
SanJose1# show ip nat translations verbose
Pro Inside global      Inside local      Outside local      Outside global
```

```
icmp 42.0.0.55:1536    192.168.0.21:1536  10.0.0.5:1536        10.0.0.5:1536
    create 00:00:29, use 00:00:26, left 00:00:33,
    flags:
extended, use_count: 0
tcp 42.0.0.55:1114     192.168.0.21:1114  10.0.0.5:21          10.0.0.5:21
    create 00:00:16, use 00:00:15, left 00:00:44,
    flags:
extended, timing-out, use_count: 0
tcp 42.0.0.55:1113     192.168.0.21:1113  10.0.0.5:23          10.0.0.5:23
    create 00:00:22, use 00:00:22, left 23:59:37,
    flags:
extended, use_count: 0
tcp 42.0.0.55:1115     192.168.0.21:1115  10.0.0.5:80          10.0.0.5:80
    create 00:00:12, use 00:00:11, left 23:59:48,
    flags:
extended, use_count: 0
```

Notice that some of the TCP transactions are using a 24-hour timeout timer. To see the other timers that you can set, use the **ip nat translation ?** command while in global configuration mode, as the following shows:

```
SanJose1(config)#ip nat translation ?
  dns-timeout    Specify timeout for NAT DNS flows
  finrst-timeout Specify timeout for NAT TCP flows after a FIN or RST
  icmp-timeout   Specify timeout for NAT ICMP flows
  max-entries    Specify maximum number of NAT entries
  port-timeout   Specify timeout for NAT TCP/UDP port specific flows
  syn-timeout    Specify timeout for NAT TCP flows after a SYN and no further
data
  tcp-timeout    Specify timeout for NAT TCP flows
  timeout        Specify timeout for dynamic NAT translations
  udp-timeout    Specify timeout for NAT UDP flows
```

The actual timeout options vary with the Cisco IOS versions. The defaults for some of the more common times are as follows:

- **dns-timeout**: Domain Name System (DNS) session (60 seconds)

- **finrst-timeout**: TCP session after a FIN or RST / end of session (60 seconds)

- **icmp-timeout**: ICMP session (60 seconds)

- **tcp-timeout**: TCP port session (86,400 seconds or 24 hours)

- **timeout**: Dynamic NAT translations (86,400 seconds or 24 hours)

- **udp-timeout**: UDP port session (300 seconds or 5 minutes)

The finrst-timeout timer makes sure that TCP sessions close the related port 60 seconds after the TCP termination sequence.

Dynamic NAT sessions can only be initiated by an internal host. It is not possible to initiate a NAT translation from outside the network. To some extent, this restriction adds a level of security to the internal network. It might also help to explain why the dynamic timeout timer for overload sessions is so short. The translation stays open just long enough to make sure that legitimate replies such as web pages, FTP and Trivial File Transfer Protocol (TFTP) sessions, and ICMP messages can get in.

In Lab 10.5.1, you saw that outside hosts can ping static NAT translations at any time, provided the inside host is up. This is so web, FTP, TFTP, DNS, and other types of servers can be shared with the outside world.

With dynamic NAT not configured for overload, the translation stays up for 24 hours. An outside host could try to access the translation and thereby get access to the host. But with the overload option, the outside host must be able to re-create the NAT IP address plus the port number. This option reduces the likelihood of an unwanted host gaining access to the system.

Step 4

To see the actual translation process and troubleshoot NAT problems, use the **debug ip nat** command and its related options.

Remember as with all debug commands, this one can seriously impair the performance of the production router and you should use it carefully. The **undebug all** command turns off all debugging.

On SanJose1, use the **debug ip nat** command to turn on the **debug** feature.

From Host A, ping the serial interface for ISP1 and observe the following translations:

```
SanJose1#debug ip nat
IP NAT debugging is on
06:37:40: NAT:  s=192.168.0.21->42.0.0.55, d=10.0.0.5 [63]
06:37:40: NAT*: s=10.0.0.5, d=42.0.0.55->192.168.0.21 [63]
06:37:41: NAT*: s=192.168.0.21->42.0.0.55, d=10.0.0.5 [64]
06:37:41: NAT*: s=10.0.0.5, d=42.0.0.55->192.168.0.21 [64]
06:37:42: NAT*: s=192.168.0.21->42.0.0.55, d=10.0.0.5 [65]
06:37:42: NAT*: s=10.0.0.5, d=42.0.0.55->192.168.0.21 [65]
06:37:43: NAT*: s=192.168.0.21->42.0.0.55, d=10.0.0.5 [66]
06:37:43: NAT*: s=10.0.0.5, d=42.0.0.55->192.168.0.21 [66]
06:38:43: NAT: expiring 42.0.0.55 (192.168.0.21) icmp 1536 (1536)
```

Notice that you can see both translations as the pings pass both ways through the NAT router. Notice that the number at the end of the row is the same for both translations of each ping. The s= indicates the source, d= indicates the destination, and -> shows the translation.

The **06:38:43** entry shows the expiration of the NAT translation.

Issue the following to turn off debugging:

```
SanJose1#undebug all
All possible debugging has been turned off
```

You can use the detailed option with **debug ip nat** to provide the port numbers as well as the IP address translations, as shown in the following:

```
SanJose1#debug ip nat detailed
IP NAT detailed debugging is on
07:03:50: NAT:  i: icmp (192.168.0.21, 1536) -> (10.0.0.5, 1536) [101]
07:03:50: NAT:  address not stolen for 192.168.0.21, proto 1 port 1536
07:03:50: NAT:  ipnat_allocate_port: wanted 1536 got 1536
07:03:50: NAT*: o: icmp (10.0.0.5, 1536) -> (42.0.0.55, 1536) [101]
07:03:51: NAT*: i: icmp (192.168.0.21, 1536) -> (10.0.0.5, 1536) [102]
07:03:51: NAT*: o: icmp (10.0.0.5, 1536) -> (42.0.0.55, 1536) [102]
07:03:52: NAT*: i: icmp (192.168.0.21, 1536) -> (10.0.0.5, 1536) [103]
07:03:52: NAT*: o: icmp (10.0.0.5, 1536) -> (42.0.0.55, 1536) [103]
07:03:53: NAT*: i: icmp (192.168.0.21, 1536) -> (10.0.0.5, 1536) [104]
07:03:53: NAT*: o: icmp (10.0.0.5, 1536) -> (42.0.0.55, 1536) [104]
```

Lab 10.5.4: Configuring TCP Load Distribution

Estimated Time: 25 Minutes

Objective

In this lab, you configure NAT with the TCP load distribution option. You also learn to use the prefix-length option as an alternative to the **netmask** option of the **ip nat pool** command. Figure 10-4 shows the sample topology for this lab.

Figure 10-4   Sample Topology for Lab 10.5.4

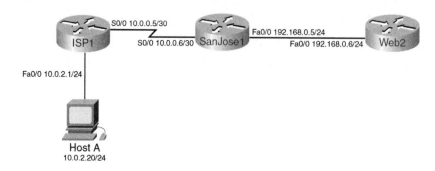

Equipment Requirements

This lab requires two routers configured as shown in Figure 10-4. Note that you cannot use a 2500 series router for this lab.

Scenario

The International Travel Agency expanded and updated its network. It chose to use the 192.168.0.0/24 private addresses and NAT to handle connectivity with the outside world. In securing the outside IP addresses from its ISP, International Travel Agency is required to pay a monthly fee for each IP address. International Travel Agency has asked you to set up a series of prototypes to test the capabilities of NAT to meet its requirements. The company hopes to be able to get by with 14 real IP addresses, 42.0.0.48/28. For a variety of reasons including security concerns, the company wants to hide the internal network from the outside.

The International Travel Agency web server, 192.168.0.5, is overwhelmed by outside traffic. You must create a pool of two mirrored servers to handle the load. You will address these servers as 192.168.0.5 and 192.168.0.6.

Outside users and DNS use the global IP address, 42.0.0.51, to access the web server. International Travel Agency would like to continue using the single address and have the NAT router distribute the requests between the two mirrored servers. You need to create a prototype that will demonstrate TCP load distribution using NAT.

Step 1

Build and configure the network according to Figure 10-4. Host A represents a user outside of the International Travel Agency network. Be sure to configure Host A with the correct default gateway.

Step 2

Issue the following to configure SanJose1 to use a default route to ISP1:

```
SanJose1(config)#ip route 0.0.0.0 0.0.0.0 10.0.0.5
```

On ISP1, issue the following to configure a static route to the global addresses used by SanJose1 for NAT:

```
ISP1(config)#ip route 42.0.0.48 255.255.255.240 10.0.0.6
```

Step 3

For testing purposes, configure SanJose1 as a web server at 192.168.0.5, as shown in the following:

```
SanJose1(config)#ip http server
```

For the purposes of this lab, another router will act as the second web server. Configure this router as shown in the following:

```
Router(config)#hostname Web2
Web2(config)#enable password cisco
Web2(config)#ip default-gateway 192.168.0.5
Web2(config)#no ip routing
Web2(config)#interface fastethernet0/0
Web2(config-if)#ip address 192.168.0.6 255.255.255.0
Web2(config-if)#no shutdown
Web2(config-if)#exit
Web2(config)#ip http server
```

Step 4

Create a NAT pool to represent the planned web servers, as the following shows:

```
SanJose1(config)#ip nat pool WebServers 192.168.0.5 192.168.0.6 prefix-length
  24 type rotary
```

Note: In this command, you use the keyword **prefix-length** instead of the keyword **netmask**. Both keywords specify the subnet mask. The **prefix-length** option lets you specify the mask as a bitcount, 24, instead of 255.255.255.0. The type rotary sets up a round-robin rotation through the designated pool. The name WebServers is a user-defined variable, so it can be any useful word.

Next, create an access list to define the global address that will be used to access the server pool. Remember that you must use 42.0.0.51. The following was the original web server IP address that is known to the outside users:

```
SanJose1(config)#access-list 50 permit 42.0.0.51
```

The following is the command that links the pool and the global address:

```
SanJose1(config)#ip nat inside destination list 50 pool WebServers
```

The **inside destination** indicates that the NAT translations will be established from the outside network to the inside network.

Issue the following to specify an interface on SanJose1 to be used by inside network hosts requiring address translation:

```
SanJose1(config)#interface fastethernet0/0
SanJose1(config-if)#ip nat inside
```

Issue the following to specify an interface as the outside NAT interface:

```
SanJose1(config)#interface serial0/0
SanJose1(config-if)#ip nat outside
```

Verify that the workstation can ping 10.0.0.5 and 10.0.0.6. Troubleshoot as necessary.

Step 5

Ping 42.0.0.51 from Host A. The ping should fail because ping uses ICMP and not TCP. TCP is the only protocol supported by the NAT load distribution feature. To test this configuration, have Host A open a web browser window.

On the address line of the web browser on Host A, enter **42.0.0.51**. When the Enter Network Password screen appears, use any username and **cisco** as the password.

Note: The password is case sensitive. If the router is not configured with **cisco** as the enable secret/password, then enter its configured password instead.

After the router is authenticated, you should see a new page.

1. What is the inside address of the router for the web server being viewed?

_____

Click the Refresh button on the web browser. A new page should appear.

2. What is the inside address of the router for the web server being viewed?

_____

3. If you click Refresh again, what will happen?

_____

Issue the **show ip nat translations** command as follows to verify that SanJose1 is distributing the TCP load to itself and Web2:

```
SanJose1#show ip nat translations
Pro Inside global        Inside local        Outside local        Outside global
tcp 42.0.0.51:80         192.168.0.5:80      10.0.2.20:1322       10.0.2.20:1322
tcp 42.0.0.51:80         192.168.0.6:80      10.0.2.20:1323       10.0.2.20:1323
tcp 42.0.0.51:80         192.168.0.5:80      10.0.2.20:1324       10.0.2.20:1324
tcp 42.0.0.51:80         192.168.0.6:80      10.0.2.20:1325       10.0.2.20:1325
tcp 42.0.0.51:80         192.168.0.5:80      10.0.2.20:1326       10.0.2.20:1326
tcp 42.0.0.51:80         192.168.0.6:80      10.0.2.20:1327       10.0.2.20:1327
tcp 42.0.0.51:80         192.168.0.5:80      10.0.2.20:1328       10.0.2.20:1328
tcp 42.0.0.51:80         192.168.0.6:80      10.0.2.20:1329       10.0.2.20:1329
tcp 42.0.0.51:80         192.168.0.5:80      10.0.2.20:1330       10.0.2.20:1330
tcp 42.0.0.51:80         192.168.0.6:80      10.0.2.20:1331       10.0.2.20:1331
tcp 42.0.0.51:80         192.168.0.5:80      10.0.2.20:1332       10.0.2.20:1332
tcp 42.0.0.51:80         192.168.0.6:80      10.0.2.20:1333       10.0.2.20:1333
```

Chapter 11

Using AAA to Scale Access Control

Lab 11.3.1: Router Security and AAA Authentication

Estimated Time: 45 Minutes

Objective

In this lab, you use the **login local** command to configure authentication and access levels. Also, you are introduced to the Cisco IOS authentication, authorization, and accounting (AAA) security authentication features, including custom prompts and debug features. Figure 11-1 shows the topology for this lab.

Figure 11-1   Sample Topology for Lab 11.3.1

Equipment Requirements

This lab requires one router and one PC to use as a host terminal, connected as shown in Figure 11-1. For this lab, you cannot use 2500 series routers.

Scenario

The International Travel Agency is concerned about the security of its routers and switches. You create a prototype of the Cisco login security features, including AAA.

Step 1

Before beginning this lab, reload the routers after erasing their startup configurations. This step prevents problems that residual configurations can cause.

Build and configure the network according to Figure 11-1. Configure the router's Fast Ethernet interface and the host's IP address, subnet mask, and default gateway. Use the following commands to configure SanJose1:

```
SanJose1(config)#enable password cisco
SanJose1(config)#line vty 0 4
SanJose1(config-line)#login
SanJose1(config-line)#password cisco
SanJose1(config-line)#line aux 0
SanJose1(config-line)#login
SanJose1(config-line)#password cisco
SanJose1(config-line)#exit
```

Verify that the router can ping the workstation.

Step 2

You can configure security for the user EXEC mode for each of the three access methods:

- VTY (Telnet)

- AUX

- Console

VTYs and AUX port access require a login password by default. If no password is set, the router does not establish a session. Instead, it returns an error message explaining that a password is required but none is set.

By default, the console port is not configured to request a login password. However, it is recommended that you configure the console port with the **login** command to enforce password security. Without it, anyone with a laptop and a console cable can easily gain access to the device.

Table 11-1 displays each of the three access methods, their associated command syntax, and a configuration example for each access method. For convenience sake, all three examples use the same password. Although it is possible to do so, the recommended practice is to set different passwords for each access method.

Table 11-1   Access Methods and Syntax for Accessing Cisco Routers

Password Type	Access Method	Syntax	Example

Console session	Console port	`line con 0`
		`password password`
		`login`
			`line con 0`
			`password cisco`
			`login`

Telnet session	VTY interfaces.
	
	The sample syntax sets all five virtual interfaces at once.
		`line vty 0 4`
		`password password`
		`login`
			`line vty 0 4`
			`password cisco`
			`login`

AUX session	AUX port
	
	If one is present, you can access it through a modem.
		`line AUX 0`
		`password password`
		`login`
			`line AUX 0`
			`password cisco`
			`login`

The **login** command requires that the user authenticate when connecting to the line. When you use the **login** command without optional keywords, you must define the password with the **password** command. You see this command in the Example column of the table.

Telnet to SanJose1 from Host A. Verify that the password, **cisco**, must be entered to gain user-level access to the router.

Step 3

It is possible to require a username as well as a password for logins to the router. Furthermore, you can configure different username/password combinations for different users. You can store these username/password combinations locally, in the database on the router, or remotely, on a specialized security server.

Configure a local username/password database for SanJose1, as follows:

```
SanJose1(config)#username remote password access
SanJose1(config)#username scott password wolfe
```

To finish the configuration, issue the login local command for line con 0, as the following shows:

```
SanJose1(config)#line con 0
SanJose1(config-line)#login local
```

The keyword **local** instructs the router to check username/password combinations against the local database. Now, users can use only the defined combinations of usernames and passwords to access the user mode from the console on the router. Like all passwords in the Cisco IOS, these passwords are case sensitive and can include text and numbers. The usernames are not case sensitive.

Exit out of the session and then log in to SanJose1 from the console port. The new access prompts look like the following:

```
User Access Verification
Username: remote
Password: access
!password does not show
SanJose1>exit

User Access Verification
Username: ScOtT
!Username is not case sensitive
Password: WoLfE
!password does not show
% Login invalid
!Used the wrong case on the password
Username: Scott
Password: wolfe
!password does not show
SanJose1>
!Used the correct case on the password
```

From Host A, Telnet to SanJose1. Confirm that the only prompt is for a password. The password **cisco** should still work.

Configure the AUX and VTYs to check username/password combinations against the local database. Enter the following commands, on SanJose1:

```
SanJose1(config)#line aux 0
SanJose1(config-line)#login local
SanJose1(config)#line vty 0 4
SanJose1(config-line)#login local
```

From Host A, Telnet to SanJose1 and authenticate using one of the locally defined username and password combinations.

Step 4

The Cisco IOS AAA feature offers several security measures. In this step, you examine the authentication feature. The AAA authentication feature validates users.

Caution: It is important to have a plan when configuring AAA because configuration commands take effect immediately. It is possible to get locked out of the router. It might be useful to issue a timed reload command without saving the current configuration. The command **reload in 20** will cause the router to automatically reload in 20 minutes and resort back to the last saved configuration.

Enter the following lines in SanJose1:

```
SanJose1(config)#aaa new-model
SanJose1(config)#username admin password aaacisco
SanJose1(config)#aaa authentication login default local enable
```

The **aaa new-model** command enables AAA. After you enter this command, the console, VTY, AUX, and TTY ports require a username and password for access.

The **aaa authentication login default** command defines how the username/password will be verified. You can use multiple options with this command. Try the first option (**local**) first. If your attempt to check a username/password using this method returns an error, you try the second method (**enable**), and so on. It is very important to note that an authentication failure is not an error. An error results only if the specified source, such as a remote server, cannot be read. The available options for the **aaa authentication login default** command are as follows:

```
SanJose1(config)#aaa authentication login default ?
  enable      Use enable password for authentication.
  group       Use Server-group
!used to access TACACS or RADIUS servers
  line        Use line password for authentication.
  Local       Use local username authentication.
  local-case  Use case-sensitive local username authentication.
```

If you configured a TACACS+ server with username/password combinations, you could configure the router with the command **aaa authentication login default group** *tacacs+* **local enable**. The **group** keyword indicates a server group, and the *tacacs+* parameter specifies the type of security server. As the second specified option in this sample command, the local database would only be used if the TACACS+ server could not be reached.

From Host A, Telnet to SanJose1. Confirm that there is a prompt for a username and password. Confirm that **admin** and **aaacisco** grant access to the router.

Disconnect from SanJose1 and then attempt to log in again. This time, verify that the username is not case sensitive but the password is.

In some cases, you might want to use case-sensitive usernames. You can configure AAA to make usernames case sensitive by adding the **local-case** option as follows:

```
SanJose1(config)#aaa authentication login default local-case enable
```

After entering this command, log out and then log back in to the router. Verify that both the username and password are now case sensitive.

Step 5

The default login prompt looks like the following:

```
User Access Verification

Username:
```

When using AAA, you have an option to present a more specific or user-friendly prompt. Issue the following command on SanJose1:

```
SanJose1(config)#aaa authentication username-prompt "Enter your NT username:"
```

To verify the new prompt, exit out of the console session and log back in.

Step 6

In this step, you examine the **debug aaa authentication** command feature. On SanJose1, activate the debug feature with the following command:

```
SanJose1#debug aaa authentication
AAA Authentication debugging is on
```

From Host A, Telnet to SanJose1. When prompted for a username, press **Enter**. The second time there is a prompt, enter a fake username/password combination. On the third and final attempt, log in correctly.

The following is a sample partial display of the **debug** output:

```
02:48:32: AAA: parse name=tty2 idb type=-1 tty=-1
02:48:32: AAA: name=tty2 flags=0x11 type=5 shelf=0 slot=0 adapter=0 port=2
channel=0
02:48:32: AAA/MEMORY: create_user (0x1FEC44) user='' ruser=''port='tty2'rem_ad
dr='192.168.0.10' authen_type=ASCII service=LOGIN priv=1
02:48:32: AAA/AUTHEN/START (1421093628): port='tty2' list=''action=LOGIN
service=LOGIN
02:48:32: AAA/AUTHEN/START (1421093628): using "default" list 02:48:32:
AAA/AUTHEN/START (1421093628): Method=LOCALCASE
02:48:32: AAA/AUTHEN (1421093628): status = GETUSER
02:48:33: AAA/AUTHEN/CONT (1421093628): continue_login (user='(undef)')
02:48:33: AAA/AUTHEN (1421093628): status = GETUSER
02:48:33: AAA/AUTHEN/CONT (1421093628): Method=LOCALCASE
02:48:33: AAA/AUTHEN/LOCAL (1421093628): no username: GETUSER
02:48:33: AAA/AUTHEN (1421093628): status = GETUSER
SanJose1#
02:48:45: AAA/AUTHEN/CONT (1421093628): continue_login (user='')
02:48:45: AAA/AUTHEN (1421093628): status = GETUSER
02:48:45: AAA/AUTHEN/CONT (1421093628): Method=LOCALCASE
02:48:45: AAA/AUTHEN (1421093628): User not found, emulating local-
override
02:48:45: AAA/AUTHEN (1421093628): status = ERROR
02:48:45: AAA/AUTHEN/START (297482216): port='tty2' list=''
action=LOGIN service
=LOGIN
```

The first four lines set up the login session. Notice that the number (1421093628) tracks the session until the failed password and a new tracking number are generated.

Note: The output might vary depending on the router platform and IOS used.

The (297482216) attempt ends up as a failed attempt or bad password, as shown in the following:

```
********Output omitted********
02:48:49: AAA/AUTHEN (297482216): password incorrect
02:48:49: AAA/AUTHEN (297482216): status = FAIL
```

The following lines are a partial display of the successful attempt:

```
********Output omitted********
02:48:57: AAA/AUTHEN/CONT (782251026): continue_login (user='bob')
02:48:57: AAA/AUTHEN (782251026): status = GETPASS
02:48:57: AAA/AUTHEN/CONT (782251026): Method=LOCALCASE
02:48:57: AAA/AUTHEN (782251026): status = PASS
```

Use **undebug all** to turn off all debugging.

Lab 11.3.2: AAA Authorization and Accounting

Estimated Time: 45 Minutes

Objective

In this lab, you use the **exec-timeout** command to control the amount of time before an idle Telnet or console session is terminated. You are also introduced to the Cisco IOS AAA security authorization and accounting features. You can implement these features to limit the EXEC commands that a user is permitted to use.

Figure 11-2 shows the sample topology in this lab.

Figure 11-2   Sample Topology for Lab 11.3.2

Equipment Requirements

This lab requires one router and one PC to use as a host terminal, connected as shown in Figure 11-2. For this lab, you cannot use 2500 series routers.

Scenario

The International Travel Agency is becoming concerned about the security of its routers and switches. You create a prototype of Cisco login security features, including AAA and Cisco Secure.

Step 1

Before beginning this lab, reload the routers after erasing their startup configurations. Configure the router's Fast Ethernet interface and the host's IP address, subnet mask, and default gateway. This step prevents problems that residual configurations might cause.

Build and configure the network according to Figure 11-2. Use the following commands to configure SanJose1:

```
SanJose1(config)#line con 0
SanJose1(config-line)#exec-timeout 0 0
SanJose1(config-line)#password cisco
SanJose1(config-line)#logging synchronous
SanJose1(config-line)#enable password cisco
SanJose1(config-line)#line vty 0 4
SanJose1(config-line)#login
SanJose1(config-line)#password cisco
SanJose1(config-line)#exec-timeout 0 0
SanJose1(config-line)#line aux 0
```

```
SanJose1(config-line)#exec-timeout 0 0
SanJose1(config-line)#login
SanJose1(config-line)#password cisco
```

The **exec-timeout 0 0** commands configure the amount of time a router waits before terminating an idle EXEC session. The first number specifies the number of minutes, and the second number specifies the number of seconds. Therefore, the command **exec-timeout 0 45** configures the idle timer to 45 seconds. Using two zeros configures the router so that the EXEC sessions never time out. Such a configuration is a security risk because unattended sessions remain open and a malicious user could potentially exploit them. Although configuring **exec-timeout 0 0** is uncommon on production routers, it is a useful configuration when performing labs.

It is possible to set different timeout values for each of the console, VTY, and AUX sessions. The default timeout for all three of these lines is 10 minutes.

Step 2

You can use the AAA feature to limit a user's options based on the username/password entered during login.

By default, there are three privilege levels on the router, as shown in Table 11-2.

Table 11-2   Three Default Privilege Levels for Routers

Privilege Level	Result
1	User level only (prompt is router>), the default level for login
15	Privileged level (prompt is router#), the level after going into enable mode
0	Seldom used, but includes five commands: **disable**, **enable**, **exit**, **help**, and **logout**

You can define levels 2 through 14 by "moving" commands from one of the default privilege levels to the new level. Configuring custom privilege levels can involve significant administration on the router.

To determine the current privilege level, type the **show privilege** command as follows:

```
SanJose1#show privilege
Current privilege level is 15
```

1.   While in user EXEC mode, what is the privilege level?

_____

2.   While in privileged EXEC mode, what is the privilege level?

_____

Configure custom privilege levels by adding the following entries to the authentication database on SanJose1:

```
SanJose1(config)#username cisco0 privilege 0 password cisco0
SanJose1(config)#username cisco15 privilege 15 password cisco15
SanJose1(config)#username cisco7 privilege 7 password cisco7
SanJose1(config)#aaa new-model
SanJose1(config)#aaa authentication login default local
```

When logging in as **cisco0**, a user only has access to the **disable**, **enable**, **exit**, **help**, and **logout** commands. When logging in as **cisco15**, a user has regular EXEC privilege access. You use the **cisco7** login to define which commands a user can access.

Note: It is important to realize that this command only creates the local database. No restrictions are applied to those usernames yet.

To prevent a lockout on the router when you start the configuration for AAA authorization, exit out completely from EXEC mode and log back into the router using the username **cisco15** and password **cisco15**.

Caution: It is important to log in as a user with privilege level 15 to modify the default privilege level of Cisco IOS commands. Failure to do so results in console session lockout when you enter the **aaa authorization exec default local** command.

After authenticating as **cisco15** and entering privilege EXEC mode, configure AAA authorization and create a custom privilege level. First, enter the following configuration command:

```
SanJose1(config)#aaa authorization exec default local
```

Next, specify which commands will be authorized. On SanJose1, issue the following commands from the console:

```
SanJose1(config)#aaa authorization commands 0 default local
SanJose1(config)#aaa authorization commands 15 default local
SanJose1(config)#aaa authorization commands 7 default local
```

After issuing these commands, a user must be "authorized" to use commands in privilege levels 0, 7, and 15.

The following is an example of the command to configure the router to query a TACACS+ server:

```
aaa authorization commands 0 default group tacacs+ local enable
```

The **group** keyword indicates a server group, and the **tacacs+** keyword indicates the type of security server. If configured with this command, the local database on SanJose1 would only be used if the TACACS+ server were unavailable.

The final step is to specify which commands will exist in privilege level 7. On SanJose1, issue the following commands from the console:

```
SanJose1(config)#privilege configure level 7 snmp-server host
SanJose1(config)#privilege configure level 7 snmp-server enable
SanJose1(config)#privilege configure level 7 snmp-server
SanJose1(config)#privilege exec level 7 ping
SanJose1(config)#privilege exec level 7 configure terminal
SanJose1(config)#privilege exec level 7 configure
```

Now, enter the **debug aaa authorization** command so you can observe the authorization process.

Step 3

From Host A, Telnet to SanJose1. Log in as **cisco15**. Because you use privilege level 15, you immediately receive privileged EXEC access.

Enter the **show privilege** command and verify the privilege level. Enter global configuration mode and then exit. Make note of the **debug** results on SanJose1's console session.

Exit out of the Telnet session.

Now, again from Host A, Telnet into the router as **cisco0**.

1.   After authenticating as **cisco0**, can you enter the privileged EXEC mode?

_____

As **cisco0**, enter the **?** command at the router prompt.

2.   How many commands are available to privilege level 0?

_____

Exit out of the Telnet session, and Telnet in as **cisco7** from Host A. Notice that this user, like **cisco15**, begins an EXEC session in privileged mode.

Enter global configuration and use the **?** command to see which commands are available in privilege level 7, as shown in the following:

```
SanJose1#config terminal

SanJose1(config)#?
Configure commands:
  default      Set a command to its defaults
  end          Exit from configure mode
  exit         Exit from configure mode
  help         Description of the interactive help system
  no           Negate a command or set its defaults
  snmp-server  Modify SNMP parameters
```

Notice the **debug** output on SanJose1. Use the **undebug all** command to turn off all debugging.

Step 4

In this step, configure AAA accounting on SanJose1. Enter privilege EXEC mode by either consoling in or Telnetting in as **cisco15**.

Note: If a TACACS+ server is not available, the results are not stored but the recording does occur.

Enter the following:

```
SanJose1(config)#aaa accounting exec default start-stop group tacacs+
SanJose1(config)#aaa accounting commands 15 default start-stop group tacacs+
SanJose1(config)#aaa accounting network default start-stop group tacacs+
SanJose1(config)#aaa accounting connection default start-stop group tacacs+
SanJose1(config)#aaa accounting system default start-stop group tacacs+
```

Table 11-3 shows a brief description of several of the commands you might encounter while configuring AAA.

Table 11-3   Table of AAA Commands

Option	Result
aaa	Identifies an AAA command
accounting	Activates the accounting or tracking feature of AAA
exec	Tracks EXEC commands on the device
commands 15	Tracks commands by privilege level 15 users; can be 0 through 15
network	Tracks network services such as PPP
connection	Tracks outbound Telnet sessions
system	Tracks system events such as reload
start-stop	Includes both Start and Stop recordings (compared to **stop-only**)
default	Uses the default list as compared to a custom list
group	Uses a group of servers
tacacs+	Uses TACACS+ instead of a RADIUS server

On SanJose1, enable **debug aaa accounting** with the following command:

```
SanJose1#debug aaa accounting
AAA Accounting debugging is on
```

From Host A, Telnet to SanJose1 and authenticate as **cisco15**. In the Telnet session, perform a couple of simple commands such as **show run**. Return to the console session on SanJose1 and examine the **debug** output. The following is a partial sample **debug** output that resulted from **cisco15** entering the **show running-config** and **copy running-config startup-config** commands:

```
01:04:59: AAA/ACCT/CMD: User cisco15, Port tty2, Priv 15:"show running-config
<cr>"
01:04:59: AAA/ACCT/CMD: Found list "default"
01:04:59: AAA/ACCT: user cisco15, acct type 3 (3901449983):
Method=tacacs+ (tacacs+)
01:05:20: AAA/ACCT/CMD: User cisco15, Port tty2, Priv 15:"copy running-config
startup-config <cr>"
01:05:20: AAA/ACCT/CMD: Found list "default"
01:05:20: AAA/ACCT: user cisco15, acct type 3 (2545785330):
Method=tacacs+ (tacacs+)
```

Note: The output might vary depending on the router platform and Cisco IOS release.

Lab 11.3.3: AAA TACACS+ Server

Estimated Time: 25 Minutes

Objective

In this lab, you configure AAA to use a TACACS+ server. Figure 11-3 shows the topology.

Figure 11-3   Sample Topology for Lab 11.3.3

Fa0/0 192.168.0.1/24

TACACS+ Server
(CiscoSecure)

Equipment Requirements

This lab requires one router and one PC to use as a host terminal, connected as shown in Figure 11-3. For this lab, you cannot use 2500 series routers.

Scenario

The International Travel Agency has set up and configured a Cisco Secure TACACS+ server. International Travel Agency needs to place the routers under the control of the TACACS+ server. You might need to modify the host name and IP address of the router.

Step 1

Before beginning this lab, reload the routers after erasing their startup configurations. This step prevents problems that residual configurations can cause.

The host shown in Figure 11-3 can be running Cisco Secure software to provide TACACS+ services. Configure SanJose1 using the following commands as an example:

```
SanJose1(config)#line con 0
SanJose1(config-line)#exec-timeout 0 0
SanJose1(config-line)#password cisco
SanJose1(config-line)#logging synchronous

SanJose1(config-line)#enable password cisco
SanJose1(config-line)#line vty 0 4
SanJose1(config-line)#login
SanJose1(config-line)#password cisco
SanJose1(config-line)#exec-timeout 0 0
SanJose1(config-line)#line aux 0
SanJose1(config-line)#exec-timeout 0 0
SanJose1(config-line)#login
SanJose1(config-line)#password cisco
```

Configure the router's Fast Ethernet interface and the host's IP address, subnet mask, and default gateway. Confirm that SanJose1 can ping the TACACS+ server.

The instructor will provide the IP address of the TACACS+ server and an encryption key. You must have this key to establish a connection between the router and the server. The instructor will also provide a username/password combination, which is already entered in the Cisco Secure database.

Step 2

On SanJose1, enter the following configuration lines:

```
SanJose1(config)#aaa new-model
SanJose1(config)#username admin password aaacisco
SanJose1(config)#aaa authentication login default group tacacs+ local enable
SanJose1(config)#tacacs-server host xxx.xxx.xxx.xxx
SanJose1(config)#tacacs-server key xxxxx
```

Note: Obtain the IP address and server key for TACACS+ or RADIUS server from your instructor.

Exit from SanJose1 and then try to log in with the username of **nobody** and the password **nothing**. This attempt should fail if there is a working connection to the TACACS+ server. If the login does not fail, reload the router and try again.

After the login using **nobody** fails, log in as the user assigned by the instructor. This login should work, indicating that SanJose1 has successfully queried the TACACS+ server and authenticated using the username and password.

1.   If you do not know any of the valid username/password combinations stored on the TACACS+ server, how can you gain access to the router?

Simulate a network outage by disconnecting the cable from the Fast Ethernet interface of router SanJose1. Attempt to log in to the router a second time through the console port.

2.   Because the attempt to query the TACACS+ server by the router will fail, which authentication method should be used? Why?

When you attempt to log in, SanJose1 tries to query the TACACS+ server first. Because the network connection to the server is unavailable, this query returns an error. The second method of authentication defined by the **aaa authentication** command specifies that the router should consult the local database next. Therefore, authentication as **admin** using the password **aaacisco** should now be available.

After you are authenticated, enter the following command on SanJose1:

```
SanJose1(config)#no username admin password aaacisco
```

3.   If no TCP/IP connection to the TACACS+ server is available, and no local username/password database exists on the router, which authentication method will be used? Why?

Exit the console session on SanJose1 and log back in again. Eventually, you see a prompt for a username. Enter the username **admin**. When prompted for a password, enter the password of

aaacisco. This authentication attempt returns an error because there is no local username/ password database. Remember, an error is not the same as an authentication failure. A failure occurs when the authentication method is operational, but the username/password combination is found to be invalid.

There is a third method of authentication defined by the **aaa authentication** command. It specifies that you should use the enable password, or secret, if it exists, if the first two authentication methods return an error.

You can access the router by using the enable password, **cisco**.

Chapter 12

Broadband Connections

There are no lab exercises for Chapter 12.

Chapter 13

Virtual Private Networks

Lab 13.8.1: Configuring a Site-to-Site IPSec VPN Using Preshared Keys

Estimated Time: 45 Minutes

Objective

In this lab, you plan and configure virtual private network (VPN) connections between two sites using Internet Key Exchange (IKE) and IP Security Protocol (IPSec). Figure 13-1 shows the sample topology for this lab.

Figure 13-1   Sample Topology for Lab 13.8.1

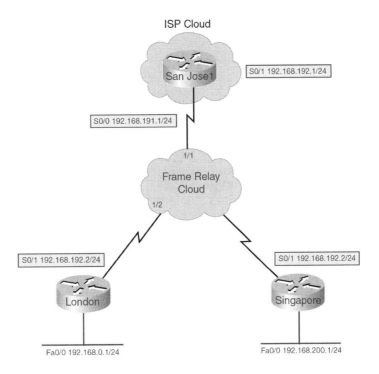

Equipment Requirements

This lab requires three routers and one Adtran or similar device, connected as shown in Figure 13-1. For this lab, you cannot use 2500 series routers.

Scenario

The International Travel Agency has decided that communications between the London and Singapore branch offices require a method of ensuring that sensitive corporate data is not being intercepted. International Travel Agency has decided to implement a site-to-site VPN solution. The solution will enable a site-to-site, IPSec-based VPN to ensure confidentiality, integrity, and authentication. In this scenario, the SanJose1 site will act as the Internet service provider (ISP).

Step 1

Before beginning this lab, you should reload each router after erasing its startup configuration. This step prevents problems that residual configurations might cause. Cable the network according to Figure 13-1. This lab assumes that you use an Adtran Atlas 550 to emulate the Frame Relay cloud. Be sure to connect the serial interfaces on the router to the port as labeled in the figure. On each router, configure its host name and Fast Ethernet address.

Note: Your results might vary depending on the routers and version of Cisco IOS.

On the SanJose1 router, configure the following:

```
SanJose1(config)#int s 0/0
SanJose1(config-if)#ip address 192.168.191.1 255.255.255.0
SanJose1(config-if)#encapsulation frame-relay
SanJose1(config-if)#frame-relay lmi-type ansi
SanJose1(config-if)#no shut

SanJose1(config)#int s 0/1
SanJose1(config-if)#ip address 192.168.192.1 255.255.255.0
SanJose1(config-if)#no shut
SanJose1(config-if)#exit

SanJose1(config)#ip route 192.168.0.0 255.255.255.0 192.168.191.2
SanJose1(config)#ip route 192.168.200.0 255.255.255.0 192.168.192.2
```

On the London and Singapore routers, configure their serial interfaces and default routes as follows:

```
London(config)#int s0/0
London(config-if)#ip add 192.168.191.2 255.255.255.0
London(config-if)#encapsulation frame-relay
London(config-if)#frame-relay lmi-type ansi
London(config-if)#no shut
London(config-if)#exit
London(config)#ip route 0.0.0.0 0.0.0.0 192.168.191.1

Singapore(config)#int s0/1
Singapore(config-if)#ip add 192.168.192.2 255.255.255.0
Singapore(config-if)#clock rate 56000
Singapore(config-if)#no shut
Singapore(config-if)#exit
Singapore(config)#ip route 0.0.0.0 0.0.0.0 192.168.192.1
```

Verify connectivity between the Fast Ethernet LANs on London and Singapore with an extended ping.

Step 2

Plan the parameters for IKE. Table 13-1 shows several of the parameters that you need to complete this configuration.

Table 13-1 Parameters Involved in Establishing IKE Between Singapore and London Routers

Parameter	Singapore Site	London Office
Key distribution method—manual or Internet Security Association and Key Management Protocol (**ISAKMP**)	isakmp	isakmp
Encryption algorithm—Data Encryption Standard (**DES**) or Triple DES (3DES)	DES	DES
Hash algorithm—Message Digest 5 (MD5) or Secure Hash Algorithm 1 (**SHA-1**)	SHA-1	SHA-1
Authentication method—Preshare or Rivest, Shamir, Adleman (**RSA**)	preshare	preshare
Key exchange—Diffie-Hellman (D-H) **Group 1** or 2	Group 1	Group 1
IKE security association (SA) Lifetime—**86400** seconds or less	86400	86400

Note: The default values are in bold.

Enable IKE on the Singapore router. Create an IKE policy with a priority of 100 using preshared keys as the method of authentication. Configure a preshared key of **cisco1234** and use the serial interface IP address on the London router as the peer's address:

```
Singapore(config)#crypto isakmp policy 100
Singapore(config-isakmp)#authentication pre-share
Singapore(config-isakmp)#crypto isakmp key cisco1234 address 192.168.191.2
```

A given preshared key is a private key shared between two peers. As a given peer, the same key could be specified to share with multiple remote peers. However, a more secure approach is to specify different keys to share between different pairs of peers.

Verify the IKE policy for the Singapore router, as follows:

```
Singapore#show crypto isakmp policy
```

The configuration output should look similar to the following:

```
Protection suite of priority 100
        encryption algorithm:   DES - Data Encryption Standard (56 bit keys).
        hash algorithm:         Secure Hash Standard
        authentication method:  Pre-Shared Key
        Diffie-Hellman group:   #1 (768 bit)
        lifetime:               86400 seconds, no volume limit
Default protection suite
        encryption algorithm:   DES - Data Encryption Standard (56 bit keys).
        hash algorithm:         Secure Hash Standard
        authentication method:  Rivest-Shamir-Adleman Signature
        Diffie-Hellman group:   #1 (768 bit)
        lifetime:               86400 seconds, no volume limit
```

Step 3

Enable IKE on the London router. Create an IKE policy with a priority of 100 using preshared keys as the method of authentication. Configure a preshared key of **cisco1234** and use the serial interface IP address on the Singapore router as the peer's address:

```
London(config)#crypto isakmp policy 100
London(config-isakmp)#authentication pre-share
London(config-isakmp)#crypto isakmp key cisco1234 address 192.168.192.2
```

Verify the IKE policy for the London router, as follows:

```
London#show crypto isakmp policy
```

The configuration output should look similar to Singapore's output.

Step 4

Plan and configure IPSec policies on the Singapore and London routers. Table 13-2 shows some of the configuration items you need to complete this task.

Table 13-2 List of Configuration Values for IPSec

Policy	Singapore	London
Transform set	esp-des	esp-des
Traffic type to be encrypted	IP	IP
SA establishment	ipsec-isakmp	ipsec-isakmp

You must configure an access list on each router to specify which traffic is to be encrypted. In this lab, you protect only the LAN traffic between sites. On the Singapore router, configure an extended access list 120 that will define this traffic going to the London router as follows:

```
Singapore(config)#access-list 120 permit ip 192.168.200.0 0.0.0.255
  192.168.0.0 0.0.0.255
```

Now, configure an IPSec transform set called MYSET and specify that DES is used to encrypt packet data. The Encapsulating Security Payload (ESP) is a security protocol that provides data privacy services, optional data authentication, and antireplay services. ESP encapsulates the data to be protected. You use ESP with DES:

```
Singapore(config)#crypto ipsec transform-set MYSET esp-des
```

Note: Up to three transform sets can be in a set. Sets are limited to one Authentication Header (AH) and up to two ESP transforms. AH is a security protocol that provides data authentication and optional antireplay services. AH is embedded in the data to be protected.

Configure an IPSec crypto map using a map name of MYMAP and a sequence number of **110**. This crypto map is to use **ipsec-isakmp**:

```
Singapore(config)#crypto map MYMAP 110 ipsec-isakmp
```

Configure the crypto map to match the access list 120, set the transform set MYSET upon the match condition, and set the peer address as the serial interface IP address on the London router, as follows:

```
Singapore(config-crypto-map)#match address 120
Singapore(config-crypto-map)#set transform-set MYSET
Singapore(config-crypto-map)#set peer 192.168.191.2
```

Finally, apply crypto map MYMAP to the serial interface on the Singapore router:

```
Singapore(config)#int s0/1
Singapore(config-if)#crypto map MYMAP
```

Use the **show crypto ipsec sa** command and verify the configuration settings:

```
Singapore#show crypto ipsec sa

interface: Serial0/1
    Crypto map tag: MYMAP, local addr. 192.168.192.2

   local  ident (addr/mask/prot/port): (192.168.200.0/255.255.255.0/0/0)
   remote ident (addr/mask/prot/port): (192.168.0.0/255.255.255.0/0/0)
   current_peer: 192.168.191.2
     PERMIT, flags={origin is acl,}
    #pkts encaps: 0, #pkts encrypt: 0, #pkts digest 0
    #pkts decaps: 0, #pkts decrypt: 0, #pkts verify 0
    #pkts compressed: 0, #pkts decompressed: 0
    #pkts not compressed: 0, #pkts compr. failed: 0, #pkts decompress failed: 0
    #send errors 0, #recv errors 0

     local crypto endpt.: 192.168.192.2, remote crypto endpt.: 192.168.191.2
     path mtu 1500, media mtu 1500
     current outbound spi: 0
********Output omitted********
```

1. Record the number of packets encrypted _____ and the number of packets decrypted _____.

Apply the similar settings to the London router as follows:

```
London(config)#access-list 120 permit ip 192.168.0.0 0.0.0.255 192.168.200.0
   0.0.0.255
London(config)#crypto ipsec transform-set MYSET esp-des
London(config)#crypto map MYMAP 110 ipsec-isakmp
London(config-crypto-map)#match address 120
London(config-crypto-map)#set transform-set MYSET
London(config-crypto-map)#set peer 192.168.192.2
```

Finally, apply crypto map MYMAP to the serial interface on the London router:

```
London(config)#int s0/0
London(config-if)#crypto map MYMAP
```

Use the **show crypto ipsec sa** command and verify the configuration settings. The output should be similar to that of the Singapore router.

Step 5

Test and verify the VPN operation. From the Singapore router, enable debugging to observe the ISAKMP and IPSec negotiation and security association creation as follows:

```
Singapore#debug crypto ipsec
Crypto IPSEC debugging is on
Singapore#debug crypto isakmp
Crypto ISAKMP debugging is on
```

Because the encryption is performed between LAN interfaces, you must use an extended ping. From the Singapore router, do an extended ping to the London router LAN interface IP address from the LAN interface IP address of the Singapore router.

1. Did you see any debug information? _____

Now, verify the security associations by using the **show crypto ipsec sa** and **show crypto isakmp sa** commands. They display the SA and ISAKMP (IKE) association tables. Output should be similar to the following:

```
Singapore#show crypto ipsec sa

interface: Serial0/1
    Crypto map tag: MYMAP, local addr. 192.168.192.2

   local  ident (addr/mask/prot/port): (192.168.200.0/255.255.255.0/0/0)
   remote ident (addr/mask/prot/port): (192.168.0.0/255.255.255.0/0/0)
   current_peer: 192.168.191.2
     PERMIT, flags={origin is acl,}
    #pkts encaps: 4, #pkts encrypt: 4, #pkts digest 0
    #pkts decaps: 4, #pkts decrypt: 4, #pkts verify 0
    #pkts compressed: 0, #pkts decompressed: 0
    #pkts not compressed: 0, #pkts compr. failed: 0, #pkts decompress failed: 0
    #send errors 1, #recv errors 0

     local crypto endpt.: 192.168.192.2, remote crypto endpt.: 192.168.191.2
     path mtu 1500, media mtu 1500
     current outbound spi: E1F92A37

     inbound esp sas:
      spi: 0xAA42D3DF(2856506335)
        transform: esp-des ,
        in use settings ={Tunnel, }
        slot: 0, conn id: 2000, flow_id: 1, crypto map: MYMAP
        sa timing: remaining key lifetime (k/sec): (4607999/3441)
        IV size: 8 bytes
        replay detection support: N
```

Complete the following information from the **show** commands:

2. Record the number of packets encrypted _____ and packets decrypted _____.

To observe the process again, clear the SAs by using the **clear crypto sa** and the **clear crypto isakmp** commands. Then, generate interesting traffic by doing additional extended pings between routers.

Notes

Notes

Notes

Notes